W9-BZA-542

Pocket

MOSCOW
& ST PETERSBURG

TOP SIGHTS • LOCAL LIFE • MADE EASY

**Mara Vorhees, Leonid Ragozin,
Simon Richmond, Regis St Louis**

In This Book

QuickStart Guide

Your keys to understanding the cities – we help you decide what to do and how to do it

Need to Know
Tips for a smooth trip

Neighbourhoods
What's where

Explore Moscow & St Petersburg

The best things to see and do, neighbourhood by neighbourhood

Top Sights
Make the most of your visit

Local Life
The insider's city

The Best of Moscow & St Petersburg

The cities' highlights in handy lists to help you plan

Best Walks
See the city on foot

Moscow & St Petersburg's Best...
The best experiences

Survival Guide

Tips and tricks for a seamless, hassle-free experience

Getting Around
Travel like a local

Essential Information
Including where to stay

Our selection of the cities' best places to eat, drink and experience:

⊙ **Sights**

✖ **Eating**

🅡 **Drinking**

✪ **Entertainment**

🅐 **Shopping**

These symbols give you the vital information for each listing:

🔎 Telephone Numbers	👪 Family-Friendly
⏱ Opening Hours	🐾 Pet-Friendly
🅿 Parking	🚍 Bus
⊖ Nonsmoking	⛴ Ferry
@ Internet Access	Ⓜ Metro
🛜 Wi-Fi Access	Ⓢ Subway
🌱 Vegetarian Selection	🚋 Tram
📖 English-Language Menu	🚂 Train

Find each listing quickly on maps for each neighbourhood:

Bar Hemingway

16 🅡 Map p233, B2

Legend has it that Hemi self, wielding a machine ...rate this timber-pan ...ered bar during ... showpiece is a ...en by Papa ar ... town. Dress ...s.com; Hôtel Rit ...; ⏱6.30pm-2a

Lonely Planet's Moscow & St Petersburg

Lonely Planet Pocket Guides are designed to get you straight to the heart of the destination.

Inside you'll find all the must-see sights, plus tips to make your visit to each one really memorable. We've split the cities into easy-to-navigate neighbourhoods and provided clear maps so you'll find your way around with ease. Our expert authors have searched out the best of the cities: walks, food, nightlife and shopping, to name a few. Because you want to explore, our 'Local Life' pages will take you to some of the most exciting areas to experience the real Moscow and St Petersburg.

And of course you'll find all the practical tips you need for a smooth trip: itineraries for short visits, how to get around, and how much to tip the guy who serves you a drink at the end of a long day's exploration.

It's your guarantee of a really great experience.

Our Promise

You can trust our travel information because Lonely Planet authors visit the places we write about, each and every edition. We never accept freebies for positive coverage, so you can rely on us to tell it like it is.

QuickStart Guide   **7**

Moscow & St Petersburg
Top Sights..................................**8**

Moscow & St Petersburg
Local Life..................................**12**

Moscow & St Petersburg
Day Planner.............................**14**

Need to Know.........................**16**

Moscow
Neighbourhoods...................**18**

St Petersburg
Neighbourhoods...................**19**

Explore   **21**

Moscow

22   Kremlin & Kitay Gorod

36   Presnya & Tverskoy

54   Arbat, Khamovniki & Zamoskvorechie

72   Meshchansky & Basmanny

St Petersburg

88   Historic Heart

106   Sennaya, Kolomna & Vasilyevsky Island

122   Smolny & Vosstaniya

134   Petrograd & Vyborg Sides

Worth a Trip:

Park Pobedy **84**
The Soviet South **146**

The Best of Moscow & St Petersburg 149

Moscow & St Petersburg's Best Walks

Moscow Metro:
Underground Art **150**

St Petersburg's
Historic Heart **152**

Moscow & St Petersburg's Best...

Museums & Galleries **154**

Imperial History **156**

Soviet History **157**

Contemporary Art **158**

Architecture **159**

Tours **160**

Eating **162**

Drinking & Nightlife **164**

Entertainment **166**

For Free **168**

For Kids **170**

Shopping **172**

Survival Guide 173

Before You Go **174**

Arriving in
Moscow **175**

Getting Around
Moscow **176**

Arriving in
St Petersburg **177**

Getting Around
St Petersburg **177**

Essential Information **178**

Language **181**

QuickStart Guide

Moscow & St Petersburg
Top Sights....................................8

Moscow & St Petersburg
Local Life....................................12

Moscow & St Petersburg
Day Planner.................................14

Need to Know.............................16

Moscow Neighbourhoods..............18

St Petersburg Neighbourhoods.........19

Welcome to Moscow & St Petersburg

Two capitals, past and present. Two urban landscapes, rich with arts, architecture, culture and dramatic histories. Yet these two cities could hardly be more different. From Moscow's red-brick fortress and Stalinist skyscrapers to St Petersburg's picturesque canals and baroque facades, the Russian capitals are a study in extraordinary but exquisite contrast.

Church of the Saviour on the Spilled Blood (p96), St Petersburg
AMOS CHAPPLE/GETTY IMAGES ©

Moscow & St Petersburg
Top Sights

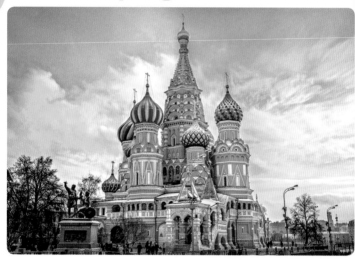

Red Square & St Basil's Cathedral
(Moscow; p28)
Majestic centrepiece of Moscow.

State Hermitage Museum
(St Petersburg; p90)
Dazzling imperial art collection and interiors.

Kremlin (Moscow; p24)

Nine centuries of Russian history.

Erarta Museum of Contemporary Art (St Petersburg; p110)

Fine contemporary Russian art.

Pushkin Museum of Fine Arts (Moscow; p56)

Russia's premier European art museum.

Gorky Park (Moscow; p58)

Communist utopia turned hipster Eden.

VOLKOVA NATALIA/SHUTTERSTOCK ©

SHCHIPKOVA ELENA/SHUTTERSTOCK ©

Church of the Saviour on the Spilled Blood (St Petersburg; p96)

Supermodel of religious architecture.

Peter & Paul Fortress (St Petersburg; p136)

Captivating island fortress.

Bolshoi Theatre (Moscow; p38)
One of the world's iconic stages.

Mariinsky Theatre
(St Petersburg; p108)
St Petersburg's grandest theatre.

Alexander Nevsky Monastery
(St Petersburg; p124)
Epicentre of St Petersburg spirituality.

Park Pobedy
(Moscow; p84)
Remembering the Great Patriotic War.

Moscow & St Petersburg Local Life

Local experiences and hidden gems to help you uncover the real cities

Red Square and Palace Square are impressive indeed. But to truly appreciate the richness of these cities, you have to get into the neighbourhoods to discover their diverse architecture, vibrant street life, atmospheric corners and unexpected oddities.

Stroll Through the Centuries
(Moscow; p40)

☑ Diverse architecture
☑ Moscow's ongoing development

Along the Stary Arbat
(Moscow; p60)

☑ Cafe-hopping and souvenir shopping
☑ Street art

Exploring Vasilevsky Island (St Petersburg; p112)
☑ Academic life ☑ Oddball museums

Discover Chkalovskaya (St Petersburg; p138)
☑ Surprising architecture ☑ Street art

The Soviet South (St Petersburg; p146)
☑ Stalinist monuments ☑ Russian ingenuity

Other great places to experience the cities like a local:

Hermitage Gardens (p46)

Chistye Prudy (p78)

Liudi Kak Liudi (p80)

Roomchik (p52)

Nevsky Prospekt (p104)

New Holland (p118)

Coffee 22 (p103)

Kirovsky Islands (p142)

Ziferblat (p131)

Griboyedov (p132)

Moscow & St Petersburg
Day Planner

Day One

Arrive at Moscow's Kremlin ticket office at 9.30am sharp (or book in advance) to reserve your time to enter the Armoury. Dedicate your morning to inspecting the ancient icons and gawking at the gold and gems in the **Kremlin** (p24). Afterwards, stroll through Alexander Garden and catch the changing of the guard at the Tomb of the Unknown Soldier. Exiting Alexander Garden, jump right into the queue on Red Square for **Lenin's Tomb** (p29) before it closes at 1pm.

Linger over lunch as long as you like, ogling the Kremlin spires and St Basil's domes. If you wish to see the interior of the **cathedral** (p29), you can do so after lunch. Otherwise, stroll through **Kitay Gorod** (p31), discovering the countless 17th-century churches and checking out Park Zaryadye (p33).

Get tickets in advance to see a show at the world-famous **Bolshoi Theatre** (p38). Afterwards, enjoy a late evening drink at **32.05** (p50) in Hermitage Garden.

Day Two

A beautiful 17th-century bell tower is the beacon that will guide you to the historic fortress of **Novodevichy Convent** (p66), which contains nearly five centuries of history. After admiring the art and architecture, head next door to the eponymous **cemetery** (p66), where many famous political and cultural figures are laid to rest.

Make your way into the **Arbat district** (p60) for an afternoon of art appreciation. Peruse the collections of the world-famous **Pushkin Museum of Fine Arts** (p56), or investigate one of the smaller niche galleries, such as the whimsical **Burganov House** (p61).

After dinner you can stroll along Moscow's most famous street – the Arbat – enjoying the talents of buskers and the atmosphere of old Moscow. If you prefer a more formal setting for your entertainment, see what's on at **Dom 12** (p70) or **Bar Strelka** (p70). Make your way to Leningrad Station in time to board your overnight train to St Petersburg.

Short on time?
We've arranged Moscow & St Petersburg's must-sees into these day-by-day itineraries to make sure you see the very best of the city in the time you have available.

Day Three

☀ Wake up in St Petersburg! Get your bearings by taking a stroll down Nevsky pr, the city's central avenue. From Moscow Station, walk west on Nevsky, cross the lovely Fontanka, drop into the **Church of the Saviour on the Spilled Blood** (p96) and end up at the dazzling ensemble on **Palace Square** (p100). Wander along the embankment to the **Summer Garden** (p101) and then back along the Moyka River.

☀ Continue along the Moyka to **St Isaac's Cathedral** (p100), visit the astonishingly elaborate interiors and then climb to the top of the dome for superb views of the city. Follow the Moyka down to the **Yusupov Palace** (p116) and the **Mariinsky Theatre** (p108), stopping to recover at the welcoming green spaces of **New Holland** (p118).

☾ If the dive bars of Dumskaya ul don't appeal, **Apotheke Bar** (p103) is a convivial spot for cocktails nearby.

Day Four

☀ After a hearty breakfast, head to the **Hermitage** (p90) and get ready for a day of artistic exhilaration. Choose which parts of the collection you want to see, though leave some room for on-the-spot decision making – the exhibition is so enormous that you'll inevitably discover something new. As well as the art, don't miss the staterooms, and allow yourself plenty of rest stops to avoid exhaustion.

☀ You may still want to spend a few hours in the museum and make the most of your day ticket. But if you leave and still have some energy, wander along before picking up a sightseeing cruise (p160) around the canals – the best way to sightsee without having to do any more walking!

☾ If you've booked ahead, dress up to spend the evening watching a ballet from the classical repertoire of the **Mariinsky Theatre** (p108). Even if you haven't booked, it's usually quite possible to buy last-minute tickets to one of the other theatres in town. For a late night drink with live jazz, drop by **Hat** (p132).

Need to Know

For more information,
see Survival Guide (p173)

Currency
rouble (₽)

Language
Russian

Visas
Required by (nearly) all; apply at least a
month in advance of your trip.

Money
ATMs widely available. Credit cards
accepted by most hotels and restaurants.

Mobile Phones
Prepaid SIM cards are readily available.
International roaming also works well.

Plugs & Adaptors
Electricity in Russia is supplied at
220v/50hz, and European-style plugs (with
two round pins) are used. A few places still
have the old 127V system.

Time
Moscow Time (GMT/UTC plus three hours)

Tipping
Tip guides around 10% of their daily rate;
a small gift will also be appreciated. At
restaurants, leave small change or 10%, if the
service warrants it. No need to tip taxi drivers.

① Before You Go

Your Daily Budget

Budget: Less than ₽1500
▶ Dorm bed: ₽600+
▶ Cafeteria meal: ₽300-500
▶ Walking tours, parks and churches: free

Midrange: ₽1500–10,000
▶ Double room at mini-hotel: ₽3500+
▶ *Prix-fixe* lunch menu: ₽400–800
▶ Museum admission: ₽200–700

Top end: More than ₽10,000
▶ Double room at luxury hotel: ₽10,000+
▶ Two-course meal with drinks: ₽2000+
▶ Ballet tickets: ₽3500

Useful Websites

Lonely Planet (www.lonelyplanet.com/
moscow) Destination information, hotel bookings, traveller forum and more.

Moscow Times (www.themoscowtimes.
com) Leading English-language newspaper
in Moscow.

Meduza (https://meduza.io) An excellent
independent source of news on Russia with
an English version.

Calvert Journal (www.calvertjournal.com)
A comprehensive site about society, culture
and travel in the 'New East', with many
Russia-specific articles.

Advance Planning

Two months before Apply for your visa.

One month before Reserve accommodation
and theatre tickets.

One week before Book guided tours.
Purchase online tickets to the Hermitage,
Kremlin and Armoury. Add useful apps such
as Google Translate and Yandex Taxi to your
smartphone.

② Arriving in Moscow & St Petersburg

✈ Moscow Airports

The three main airports (**Sheremetyevo**, **Domodedovo** and **Vnukovo**) are accessible by the convenient **Aeroexpress Train** (☎8-800-700 3377; www.aeroexpress.ru; one way ₽420; ⊙6am-midnight), which takes 35 to 45 minutes to the city centre. Otherwise, book an official airport taxi through the dispatcher counter (₽2000 to ₽2500). If you order a taxi by phone or with a mobile-phone app it will be about 50% cheaper.

✈ Pulkovo International Airport

From St Petersburg's superb airport (www. pulkovoairport.ru), an official taxi to the centre should cost between ₽800 and ₽1000; if you book one via an app it's likely to be ₽700. Alternatively, take bus 39 (35 minutes) or 39A (20 minutes) to Moscow Station.

🚃 Train Stations

Rail riders will arrive at one of the central train stations in Moscow and/or St Petersburg. All of the train stations are located in the city centre, with easy access to the metro. Alternatively, most taxi companies offer a fixed rate of ₽400 to ₽600 for a train-station transfer.

③ Getting Around

Ⓜ Metro

The metro systems in both cities are cheap, efficient, interesting to look at and easy to use. The downside is that they can be uncomfortably crowded during peak periods. The metro runs from approximately 5.45am to 12.45am in St Petersburg, 5.30am to 1.30am in Moscow.

🚌 Bus

Buses are best for shorter distances in areas without good metro coverage, especially in St Petersburg.

🚗 Taxi

Well-marked 'official' taxi cabs do not roam the streets looking for fares but you can book a taxi using an app or an official agency.

🚶 Walk

Distances can be vast, but Moscow and St Petersburg are surprisingly walkable cities, especially in the centre. Use the underground crosswalk when crossing busy streets.

🚲 Bike

Cycling on the streets can be dangerous, but it's getting better. In any case, cycling is a pleasant way to get around if you stick to the routes along the river and in the city parks. Bikes are available from the bike-share programs: **VeloBike** (www.velobike. ru) in Moscow and **Velogorod** (http://spb. velogorod.org) in St Petersburg.

Moscow
Neighbourhoods

Meshchansky & Basmanny (p72)
Galleries and quirky shops fill revamped factories, near ul Pokrovka's enticing restaurants.

⊙ Top Sight
Winzavod & ArtPlay

Presnya & Tverskoy (p36)
Lush parks, spangled churches and noteworthy architecture, with some worthwhile unusual museums.

⊙ Top Sight
Bolshoi Theatre

Worth a Trip
⊙ Top Sight
Park Pobedy (p84)

Bolshoi
Theatre ⊙

Red Square
& St Basil's
Cathedral

Winzavod
& ArtPlay ⊙

Kremlin ⊙ ⊙

Pushkin ⊙
Museum of
Fine Arts

⊙ Park
Pobedy

⊙ Gorky
Park

Arbat, Khamovniki & Zamoskvorechie (p54)
Museums and galleries, plus Novodevichy Convent and lively Gorky Park, span the river.

⊙ Top Sights
Pushkin Museum of Fine Art

Gorky Park

Kremlin & Kitay Gorod (p22)
Packed with historic sights and church-lined streets, plus Park Zaryadye, steps from Red Square.

⊙ Top Sights
Kremlin

Red Square & St Basil's Cathedral

St Petersburg
Neighbourhoods

Worth a Trip
○ **Local Life**
The Soviet South (p146)

Petrograd & Vyborg Sides (p134)
These northern islands offer swathes of greenery and a smattering of museums.

◉ **Top Sight**
Peter & Paul Fortress

Smolny & Vosstaniya (p122)
Museums, underground art and lively bars, from Fontanka River to Alexander Nevsky Monastery.

◉ **Top Sight**
Alexander Nevsky Monastery

Peter & Paul Fortress
◉

Erarta Museum of Contemporary Art
◉

State Hermitage Museum
◉

◉ ◉ *Church of the Saviour on the Spilled Blood*

◉
Mariinsky Theatre

Alexander Nevsky Monastery
◉

Sennaya, Kolomna & Vasilyevsky Island (p106)
Waterways weave around grand palaces and theatres, with classical buildings and museums on Vasilyevsky Island.

◉ **Top Sights**
Mariinsky Theatre
Erarta Museum of Contemporary Art

Historic Heart (p88)
Sparkling churches, picturesque bridges and parks, and the city's showstopper – the Hermitage Museum.

◉ **Top Sights**
State Hermitage Museum
Church of the Saviour on the Spilled Blood

Explore
Moscow

Kremlin & Kitay Gorod 22

Presnya & Tverskoy 36

Arbat, Khamovniki
& Zamoskvorechie 54

Meshchansky & Basmanny 72

Worth a Trip

Park Pobedy 84

Resurrection Gate, Red Square (p28)
MARCO RUBINO/SHUTTERSTOCK ©

Explore

Kremlin & Kitay Gorod

Red Square and the Kremlin are the historic, geographic and spiritual heart of Moscow, as they have been for nearly 900 years. The mighty fortress, the iconic onion domes of St Basil's Cathedral and the granite mausoleum of Vladimir Ilych Lenin are among the city's most important historic sights. This is the starting point for any visit to Moscow.

The Sights in a Day

☀ If you have only one day in Moscow, you will probably spend it here. Buy your tickets in advance (online) to visit the churches and monuments of the **Kremlin** (p24), including the impressive museum in the **Armoury** (p26). Catch the changing of the guard at the **Tomb of the Unknown Soldier** (p27) on your way out.

☀ Have lunch in Soviet style at **Stolovaya No 57** (p34) or enjoy Kremlin views from **Bosco Cafe** (p34). Spend the afternoon marvelling at the splendour of **Red Square** (p28), including **St Basil's Cathedral** (p29) and **Lenin's Mausoleum** (p29). (Note that if you want to go inside the mausoleum to see Lenin in person, you'll have to come here first, due to the early closing time.) Get lost in the urban wilds of the new **Park Zaryadye** (p31).

☾ Indulge in a meaty dinner from **Ryby Net** (p33), or **Farsh** (p32) for something more casual. Afterwards, the ancient streets of **Kitay Gorod** (p31) are worth a wander, ending at Red Square (one last time) to see this impressive ensemble under the lights.

 Top Sights

Kremlin (p24)

Red Square (p28) & St Basil's Cathedral (p29)

 Best of Kremlin & Kitay Gorod

Drinking
Jawsspot Msk (p34)

Mandarin Combustible (p34)

Museums & Galleries
Armoury (p26)

Park Zaryadye Pavilion (p31)

Churches & Monasteries
St Basil's Cathedral (p29)

Kremlin (p24)

Parks & Gardens
Park Zaryadye (p33)

Alexander Garden (p27)

Getting There

Ⓜ **Metro** Three metro lines converge at Red Square. Okhotny Ryad station is line 1 (red); Teatralnaya is line 2 (dark green); and Ploshchad Revolyutsii is line 3 (dark blue). Lines 6 and 7 (orange and purple) intersect at Kitay Gorod station. Line 1 (red) has an eponymous station at Lubyanka, which is also useful for Kitay Gorod.

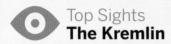

Top Sights
The Kremlin

The apex of Russian political power and once the centre of the Orthodox Church, the Kremlin is not only the kernel of Moscow but of the whole country. From here, autocratic tsars, communist dictators and modern-day presidents have done their best – and worst – for Russia. These red-brick walls and tent-roof towers enclose 800 years of artistic accomplishment, religious ceremony and political clout.

Кремль

◉ Map p30, B4

www.kreml.ru

₽500

⊙10am-5pm Fri-Wed, ticket office 9.30am-4.30pm Fri-Wed

Ⓜ Aleksandrovsky Sad

Patriarch's Palace

Built for Patriarch Nikon mostly in the mid-17th century, the highlight of the Patriarch's Palace (Патриарший дворец) is perhaps the ceremonial Cross Hall (Крестовая палата), where the tsar's and ambassadorial feasts were held. From here you can access the five-domed Church of the Twelve Apostles (Церковь двенадцати апостолов), which has a gilded, wooden iconostasis and a collection of icons by leading 17th-century icon painters.

Assumption Cathedral

On the northern side of Sobornaya pl, with five golden helmet domes and four semicircular gables facing the square, the Assumption Cathedral (Успенский собор) is the focal church of pre-revolutionary Russia and the burial place of most of the heads of the Russian Orthodox Church from the 1320s to 1700. A striking 1660s fresco of the Virgin Mary faces Sobornaya pl, above the door once used for royal processions. If you have limited time, come straight here. The visitors' entrance is at the western end.

Ivan the Great Bell Tower

With its two golden domes rising above the eastern side of Sobornaya pl, the **Ivan the Great Bell Tower** (Колокольня Ивана Великого; ₽250; ◷10am-5pm Apr-Oct) is the Kremlin's tallest structure – a landmark visible from 30km away. Before the 20th century it was forbidden to build any higher than this tower in Moscow. Purchase a ticket for a specifically timed admission to climb the 137 steps to the top for sweeping views. The infamous Tsar Cannon (Царь-пушка) and Tsar Bell (Царь-колокол) are nearby.

☑ Top Tips

▶ Visitors are allowed to enter the Armoury only at specified times (10am, noon, 2.30pm and 4.30pm).

▶ Visitors can only enter Ivan the Great Bell Tower at specified times (10.15am, 11.15am, 1pm, 2pm, 3pm and 4pm).

▶ Full-price Armoury tickets are available for advance online purchase. Otherwise, tickets go on sale 45 minutes prior to each session. Be at the ticket window when sales begin, tickets are limited.

▶ Photography is not permitted inside the Armoury or in any of the buildings on Sobornaya pl (Cathedral Sq).

✕ Take a Break

There's no place to eat inside the Kremlin walls, but you'll find some food trucks serving sandwiches, hot dogs and ice cream in Alexander Garden.

For a proper, sit-down meal, head to Gran Cafe Dr Zhivago (p47).

Archangel Cathedral

The Archangel Cathedral (Архангельский собор) at the southeastern corner of Sobornaya ploshchad was for centuries the coronation, wedding and burial church of tsars. It was built by Ivan Kalita in 1333 to commemorate the end of the great famine, and dedicated to Archangel Michael, guardian of the Moscow princes. It contains the tombs of almost all of Muscovy's rulers from the 14th to the 17th century.

Annunciation Cathedral

The Annunciation Cathedral (Благовещенский собор), at the southwest corner of Sobornaya pl, contains impressive murals in the gallery and an archaeology exhibit in the base-ment. The central chapel contains the celebrated icons of master painters Theophanes the Greek and Andrei Rublyov.

Armoury

The **Armoury** (Оружейная палата; adult/child ₽700/free; ⊘tours 10am, noon, 2.30pm & 4.30pm Fri-Wed) dates back to 1511, when it was founded under Vasily III to manufacture and store weapons, imperial arms and regalia for the royal court. Later it also produced jewellery, icon frames and embroidery. During the reign of Peter the Great all craftspeople, goldsmiths and silversmiths were sent to St Petersburg, and the Armoury became a mere museum storing the royal treasures. To this day, the Armoury still contains plenty

The Kremlin

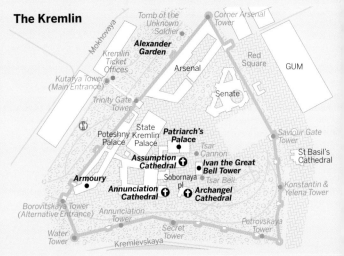

Tsar Bell (p25)

of treasures for ogling, and remains a highlight of any visit to the Kremlin.

If possible, buy your ticket to the Armoury when you buy your ticket to the Kremlin. Your ticket will specify a time of entry. A one-hour audio guide is available to point out some of the highlights of the collection.

Alexander Garden

The first public park in Moscow, Alexander Garden (Александровский сад) sits along the Kremlin's western wall. Colourful flower beds and impressive Kremlin views make it a favourite strolling spot for Muscovites and tourists alike.

The Tomb of the Unknown Soldier (Могила неизвестного солдата) contains the remains of one soldier who died in December 1941 at Km41 of Leningradskoe sh – the nearest the Nazis came to Moscow. It is a kind of national pilgrimage spot, where newlyweds bring flowers and have their pictures taken. The inscription reads: 'Your name is unknown, your deeds immortal'. Every hour on the hour, the guards perform a perfectly synchronized ceremony to change the guards on duty.

Top Sights
Red Square & St Basil's Cathedral

One's first time setting foot on Red Square is a guaranteed awe-striker. The vast rectangular stretch of cobblestones is surrounded by architectural marvels, including St Basil's Cathedral. This panorama never fails to send the heart aflutter, especially at night. Furthermore, it evokes an incredible sense of import to stroll across the place where so much of Russian history has unfolded.

Красная площадь

👁 Map p30, B3 and C4

Krasnaya pl

Ⓜ Ploshchad Revolyutsii

St Basil's Cathedral

St Basil's Cathedral

At the southern end of Red Square stands the icon of Russia: **St Basil's Cathedral** (Покровский собор, Храм Василия Блаженного; adult/student ₽350/150; ⊘ticket office 11am-5pm Nov-Apr, to 6pm May-Oct). This crazy confusion of colours, patterns and shapes is the culmination of a style that is unique to Russian architecture. In 1552 Ivan the Terrible captured the Tatar stronghold of Kazan on the Feast of Intercession. He commissioned this landmark church, officially the Intercession Cathedral, to commemorate the victory. Created from 1555 to 1561, this masterpiece would become the ultimate symbol of Russia.

Lenin's Mausoleum

Although Vladimir Ilych requested that he be buried beside his mum in St Petersburg, he still lies in state at the foot of the Kremlin wall in this **mausoleum** (Мавзолей Ленина; www.lenin.ru; Krasnaya pl; admission free; ⊘10am-1pm Tue-Thu, Sat & Sun), receiving visitors who come to pay their respects. Line up at the western corner of the square (near the entrance to Alexander Garden) to see the embalmed leader, who has been here since 1924. Note that photography is not allowed and stern guards ensure that all visitors remain respectful and silent.

Saviour Gate Tower

The Kremlin's 'official' exit onto Red Square is the stately red-brick Saviour Gate Tower (Спасская башня). This gate – considered sacred – has been used for processions since tsarist times. The two white-stone plaques above the gate commemorate the tower's construction in 1491. The current clock was installed in the gate tower in the 1850s. Hauling 3m-long hands and weighing 25 tonnes, the clock takes up three of the tower's 10 levels.

☑ Top Tips

▶ For an excellent photo op with good selfie potential, go around to the south side of St Basil's Cathedral, where there are unimpeded views and fewer people.

▶ Red Square empties out at night, but this is when the square is most atmospheric.

▶ The square is often closed for various celebrations or their rehearsals, so allow some leeway in your schedule.

✕ Take a Break

There are other choices inside GUM, but the mall's Bosco Cafe (p34) is the only eatery that is right on Red Square.

Alternatively, stroll down to the end of Nikolskaya ul for an affordable lunch at Bon App Cafe (p33).

Georgievsky per

Teatralnaya pl

Teatralnaya Ⓜ

Teatralny proezd

Pl Revolyutsii

Okhotny Ryad

Okhotny Ryad

Tverskaya ul

Okhotny Ryad Ⓜ

Okhotny Ⓜ Ryad

Okhotny Ryad Ⓜ

pl Revolyutsii

Ploshchad Revolyutsii Ⓜ

Manezhnaya pl

Manezhnaya ul

Nikolskaya ul

Moscow Free Tour 4

CITY CENTRE

Ploshchad Revolyutsii Ⓜ

Bogoyavlensky per

Lubyanka Ⓜ

Lubyanka Ⓜ Lubyanskaya pl

Myasnitskaya u

Tretyakovsky proezd

7 Ⓧ

Ⓧ 5

Maly Cherkassky per

9 Ⓧ Ⓧ 6

Bolshoy Cherkassky per

Lubyansky proezd

Novaya pl

Starop per

Kitay Gorod

Kitay Goro

State History Museum 3 Ⓞ

8 Ⓧ

10 Ⓐ

GUM

Kitay Gorod Ⓞ 1

KITAY GOROD

Ibatye

Nikolsky per

Corner Arsenal Tower

St Nicholas Tower

Lenin's Mausoleum

Senate Tower

Red Square Ⓞ

Vetoshny per

ul Ilynka

Rybny per

Rybny per

Alexander Garden

Arsenal

Trinity Gate Tower

Kremlin Ⓞ

Borovitskaya Gate Tower

St Basil's Cathedral Ⓞ

Alarm Tower

Khrustalny per

ul Varvarka

Moskvoretskaya ul

Gostiny Dvor

ul Varvarka

Poteshny Palace

Tsar Cannon

Terem Palace

Hall of Facets

Ivan the Great Bell Tower

Konstantin & Yelena Tower

2 Ⓞ

Park Zaryadye Pavilion

Park Zaryadye

State Kremlin Palace

Sobornaya pl (Cathedral Square)

Secret Tower

Kremlevskaya nab

Moskvoretskaya Tower

Annunciation Tower

Moscow River

Sofiyskaya nab

Bolshoy Moskvoretsky Most

For reviews see	
Ⓞ Top Sights	p.
Ⓞ Sights	p
Ⓧ Eating	p.
Ⓔ Drinking	p.
Ⓐ Shopping	p.

Ⓝ

0   200
0   0.1 mile

Viewing platform, Park Zaryadye

Sights

Kitay Gorod

AREA

1 ◉ Map p30, D3

This 13th-century neighbourhood was the first in Moscow to grow up outside the Kremlin walls. While its name means 'China Town' in modern Russian, do not expect anything Chinese – the name derives from an old Russian word meaning 'wattle', for the supports used for the walls that protected the suburb. This is the heart of medieval Moscow and parts of the neighbourhood's walls are visible. The main places of interest are the collection of churches, especially along ul Varvarka, and the new Park Zaryadye (p33).

Park Zaryadye Pavilion

MUSEUM

2 ◉ Map p30, C4

This glass-dome pavilion was the first element of Park Zaryadye to open to the public. A creation of Sergei Kuznetsov, the pavilion was designed as an 'observation deck' for the ongoing work on the park. Construction was not actually visible from the pavilion; rather, the central chamber is wallpapered in QR codes – a surprisingly appealing look – that contain maps, designs, photographs and other information about the new park. At the entrance, visitors receive tablets which they can use to decode the electronic exhibits. (Павильон парка "Зарядье"; Moskvoretskaya ul; admission free)

Interior, State History Museum

State History Museum   MUSEUM

3 ◉ Map p30, B3

At the northern end of Red Square, the State History Museum has an enormous collection covering Russian history from the time of the Stone Age. Dating from the late 19th century, it is itself an attraction – each room is in the style of a different period or region, some with highly decorated walls echoing old Russian churches. (Государственный исторический музей; www.shm.ru; Krasnaya pl 1; adult/student ₽350/100, audio guide ₽300; ⊘ ticket office 10am-5pm Mon, Wed, Thu & Sun, to 9pm Fri & Sat; Ⓜ Okhotny Ryad)

Moscow Free Tour   WALKING

4 ◉ Map p30, B2

Every day these enthusiastic ladies offer an informative, inspired 2½-hour guided walk around Red Square and Kitay Gorod – and it's completely free. It's so good that (they hope) you'll sign up for one of their excellent paid tours, covering the Kremlin, the Arbat and the Metro, or themes such as communist Moscow. (✆ 495-222 3466; www.moscowfreetour.com; Nikolskaya ul 4/5; guided walk free, paid tours from €31)

Eating

Farsh   BURGERS $

5 ✕ Map p30, C1

Burger mania is sweeping the capital and Farsh is at the forefront, serving gourmet burgers and amazing French fries, as well as chicken wings, barbecue ribs and grilled steaks. This is the equally tasty fast-food counterpart to neighbouring Ryby Net, except it's not always that fast during busy times. (Фарш; ✆ 495-258 4205; www.farsh burger.ru; Nikolskaya ul 12; burgers ₽250-580; ⊘ 10am-midnight; Ⓜ Lubyanka)

Grand Coffee Mania   CAFE $$

6 ✕ Map p30, D1

This place has the same overpriced but appetizing fare as other outlets of the ubiquitous chain, but the fabulous 'grand cafe' interior makes this one a special experience. Marble floors, art-deco chandeliers and elaborate latticework evoke another era. Efficient service and excellent atmosphere. (Кофе мания; ☎495-960 2295; www.coffeemania.ru; Mal Cherkassky per 2; breakfast ₽300-500, mains ₽500-1200; ⊙8am-midnight Mon-Thu, to 2am Fri, 10am-2am Sat, 10am-midnight Sun; ❄🛜✐; Ⓜ Lubyanka)

Bon App Cafe
EUROPEAN $$

7 🍴 Map p30, C1

On the ground floor of the Nautilus shopping centre, this is a popular lunch spot for workers, shoppers and tourists recovering from Red Square. The interior is cool and contemporary, but still comfortable. The wide-ranging menu includes pizza, pasta and other Russian and European fare, so there is something for everyone. (www.facebook.com/bonappcafe; 1st fl, Nikolskaya ul 25; pizza & pasta ₽420-480, mains ₽480-840; ⊙9am-midnight Mon-Fri, from 11am Sat & Sun; 🛜✐; Ⓜ Lubyanka)

Ryby Net
STEAK $$$

If you don't get the name, which means 'No Fish', the sides of beef hanging in the window should give you a clue. This is where you come (see 5 🍴 Map 30, C1) to get your carnavore on. Steaks are prepared from top-quality marbled meat and served with a fresh-baked baguette. There's a good wine list and custom cocktails to

---

Understand
Park Zaryadye
- - - - - - - - - - - - - - - - - - - -

For the first time in 50 years, Moscow is getting a major new park, and it's happening in the heart of the historic centre – just a few steps from Red Square.

Park Zaryadye occupies a prominent site along the Moscow River, wedged into historic Kitay Gorod. It was designed by the New York firm Diller Scofidio & Renfro (DS&R), which is renowned for its use of 'wild urbanism', a technique that merges the historic city streets with wild natural habitats.The 13 hectares include four different areas representing Russia's geographic zones – tundra, steppe, forest and wetlands – flowing seamlessly into each other. The most anticipated feature, perhaps, is a sort of bridge to nowhere, which will stretch out across Moskvoretskaya nab and over the Moscow River, then loops back to Zaryadye.

In addition to the parkland, Zaryadye will contain a vast outdoor amphitheatre and several new museums, built into the hillsides and showcasing Russia's natural resources and richness. The Park Zaryadye Pavilion (p31) serves as a museum of Park Zaryadye, providing an overview of the park and its development.

accompany. (Рыбы Нет; ☏495-258 4206; www.novikovgroup.ru; Nikolskaya ul 12; mains ₽800-2000; ⏱noon-midnight; Ⓜ Lubyanka)

Bosco Cafe

ITALIAN $$$

8 Map p30, B3

Sip a cappuccino in view of the Kremlin. Munch on lunch while the crowds line up at Lenin's Mausoleum. Enjoy an afternoon aperitif while admiring St Basil's domes. Service is lacking and the menu is overpriced, but this cafe on the ground floor of the GUM mall is the only place to sit right on Red Square and marvel at its magnificence. (☏495-620 3182; https://gumrussia.com/cafe/bosco-cafe; GUM, Krasnaya pl 3; pasta ₽500-1000, mains ₽1200-2000; ⏱10am-10pm; Ⓜ Ploshchad Revolyutsii)

Top Tip

Stolovaya No 57

Newly minted, this old-style **cafeteria** (Столовая 57; ☏495-620 3129; https://gumrussia.com/shops/stolovaya-57; 3rd fl, GUM, Krasnaya pl 3; mains ₽200-300; ⏱10am-10pm; Ⓜ Okhotny Ryad) inside GUM offers a nostalgic re-creation of dining in post-Stalinist Russia. The food is good – and cheap for such a fancy store. Meat cutlets and cold salads come highly recommended. This is a great place to try 'herring in a fur coat' (herring, beetroots, carrots and potatoes).

Drinking

Mandarin Combustible

LOUNGE

9 📍 Map p30, D1

Dining, drinking and dancing are all on offer in this sexy space. There is a long menu of Pan Asian cuisine – as well as sushi, pasta, tapas and more – served all night long for Moscow's nonstop party people. Drinks are forgettable and service is slack, but everything (and everyone) looks fine – and sometimes that's what matters. (☏495-745 0700; Mal Cherkassky per 2; ⏱noon-6am; 🛜; Ⓜ Lubyanka)

Jawsspot Msk

CRAFT BEER

On the top floor of the Nautilus shopping centre (see 7 ✕ Map32, C1), you'll find this small surfer beer bar. An even smaller terrace gives a fantastic view of Lubyanskaya pl. Jawsspot hails from the Urals, where they've been brewing beer in a former laundry since 2008. Now they're serving their great-tasting, cleverly named brews in the capital. (http://tinyurl.com/yc9wcakx; 6th fl, Nautilus, Nikolskaya ul 25; ⏱noon-midnight Sun-Thu, to 2am Fri & Sat; 🛜; Ⓜ Lubyanka)

Shopping

GUM

MALL

10 🔒 Map p30, B3

Behind its elaborate 240m-long facade on the northeastern side of Red Square, GUM is a bright, bustling

GUM

shopping mall with hundreds of fancy stores and restaurants. With a skylight roof and three-level arcades, the spectacular interior was a revolutionary design when it was built in the 1890s, replacing the Upper Trading Rows that previously occupied this site.

Pronounced 'goom', the initials GUM originally stood for the Russian words for 'State Department Store'. When it was privatised in 2005, the name was officially changed to 'Main Department Store'. Fortunately, the words for 'state' and 'main' both start with a Russian 'G'. (ГУМ; www.gum.ru; Krasnaya pl 3; ⊘10am-10pm; M Ploshchad Revolyutsii)

Explore

Presnya & Tverskoy

Tverskoy is Moscow's busiest commercial district. Few people can afford to live here, but millions pour in daily to work, shop or dine out. It is also home to 20-plus theatres and several renowned galleries. To the west, the Presnya district's ample attractions include its impressive and varied architecture and several noteworthy literary sites.

The Sights in a Day

☀ Start your exploration at the majestic Teatralnaya pl (Theatre Sq), home to the world-famous **Bolshoi Theatre** (pictured left; p38). Wander up Bolshaya Dmitrovka toward the Boulevard Ring, shopping the boutiques, trying your hand at some **Soviet arcade games** (p44) and taking frequent stops for people-watching and latte-sipping from Moscow's many sidewalk cafes. For more serious sight-seeing, browse an exhibit at the **Moscow Museum of Modern Art** (p44).

☀ After lunch, you can investigate one of many excellent museums (most of which require a metro ride). Take your pick from the state-of-the-art **Jewish Museum & Centre of Tolerance** (p45), the sobering **Gulag History Museum** (p46) or the massive **Central Museum of the Armed Forces** (p45).

☾ Tverskoy and Presnya are home to Moscow's most venerable cultural institutions. For the evening, get tickets to a ballet at the **Bolshoi** (p38), a concert at the **Tchaikovsky Conservatory** (p52) or an experimental show at the **Stanislavsky Electrotheatre** (p51). Alternatively, dinner at the **Cafe Pushkin** (p48) is always a treat.

For a local's day in Presnya, see p40.

◉ **Top Sights**

Bolshoi Theatre (p38)

◯ **Local Life**

Stroll through the Centuries (p40)

♥ **Best of Presnya & Tverskoy**

Eating

Delicatessen (p47)

Cafe Pushkin (p48)

Khachapuri (p47)

Drinking

Glavpivmag (p51)

32.05 (p50)

Delicatessen (p47)

Cafe Mart (p50)

Getting There

Ⓜ **Metro** Both Tverskoy and Presnya are accessible by metro stops along the green Zamoskvoretskaya line, including Teatralnaya, Tverskaya and Mayakovskaya. Most of these stops are accessible from intersecting lines.

Ⓜ **Metro** For the more western parts of the Presnya, the most useful metro stations are at Kudrinskaya pl: Barrikadnaya on line 7 and Krasnopresnenskaya on line 5 (ring line).

Top Sights
Bolshoi Theatre

The Bolshoi is still one of Moscow's most romantic and entertaining options for a night on the town. The glittering six-tier auditorium has an electric atmosphere, evoking over 240 years of premier music and dance. Both ballet and opera are on offer.

Большой театр

◉ Map p42, D7

www.bolshoi.ru

Teatralnaya pl 1

tickets ₽100-12,000

🕓 closed late Jul–mid-Sep

Ⓜ Teatralnaya

Interior

Theatre

The present pink-and-white beauty was built in 1824, and saw the premiers of Tchaikovsky's *Swan Lake* in 1877 and *The Nutcracker* in 1919. The facade is famed for the bronze troika that is seemingly about to fly off the front. Gracing Teatralnaya Sq, the fountain by Vitali, which features bronze sculptures of the three muses, is Moscow's oldest. A welcome supplement, Bolshoi's new stage was opened next door in 2002.

Repertoire & Direction

Opera and ballet directors come and go, leaving their imprint on the repertoire and generating controversy. But classic gems, such as the iconic *Swan Lake* and *Boris Godunov*, remain. There have been successful experiments with 20th-century and modern music in recent years, but they don't tend to linger for long.

Since 2016, the Bolshoi has been operating under the artistic direction of Makhar Vaziev, a former Mariinsky director and a self-proclaimed autocrat. Vaziev promises to implement a well-practised strategy of promoting young talent and experimenting with innovative programming.

Scandal

Juicy stories about the Bolshoi's singers and ballerinas regularly appear in tabloids. In the last two decades, the Bolshoi has been marred by politics, scandal and even outright crime.

And yet, the show must go on – and it will.

☑ Top Tips

▶ Purchase tickets online at www.bolshoi.ru/en/timetable before you set off on your trip to Moscow

▶ Dress to the nines so you can blend into the jet-set crowd.

▶ Come early to explore the richly decorated building.

▶ Have a ritual glass of bubbly in the buffet, a great place for people watching.

✕ Take a Break

If you've decided to splash out on a Bolshoi ticket, splash it all the way! Brasserie Most (p48) is a suitably ritzy place for a pre-theatre dinner.

There are cafes inside both Bolshoi buildings, but you may have to queue to get your prosecco.

Local Life
Stroll Through the Centuries

The vast, diverse Presnya district spans the centuries, with a remarkable blend of building styes from from the last three. Walk from the past into the present (and beyond) - and get a glimpse of the future, as well.

❶ Boulevard Stroll
From Pushkinskaya pl, stroll south along Tverskoy bul. This is the loveliest stretch of the Boulevard Ring, lined with grand architecture, blooms and a statue of poet Sergei Yesenin.

❷ Art Nouveau Beauty
The fascinating 1906 **Ryabushinsky Mansion** (Особняк Рябушинского; Malaya Nikitskaya ul 6/2; adult/student ₽400/150; ⊙11am-5.30pm Wed-Sun; Ⓜ Pushkinskaya)

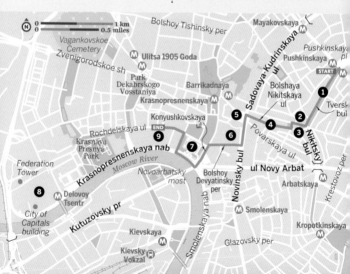

was designed by architect Fyodor Shekhtel and gifted to celebrated author Maxim Gorky in 1931. The house is a visual fantasy with ceiling murals, stained glass, and exterior tilework.

❸ Ill-Fated Affair

In 1831 poet Alexander Pushkin married artist Natalia Goncharova in the elegant **Church of the Grand Ascension** (Храм Большое Вознесение у Никитских Ворот; http://bolshoevoznesenie.ru; pl Nikitskie Vorota; ⊙8am-6pm), on the western side of pl Nikitskie Vorota. Six years later he died in St Petersburg, defending her honour in a duel. Such passion, such romance...

❹ Imperial Grandeur

Bolshaya Nikitskaya ul is studded with elegant mansions. Some of the most striking include the elaborate facade at No 51 and the tiled edifice of Lopatina Building at No 54.

❺ Stalinist Skyscraper

Kudrinskaya pl is dominated by a massive skyscraper (one of Stalin's 'Seven Sisters'). The 160m, 22-storey **structure** (Высотка на Кудринской площади; Kudrinskaya pl 1; Ⓜ Barrikadnaya) contains elite apartments, mostly occupied by preeminent cultural figures during Soviet times.

❻ Modernist Landmark

A model for Le Corbusier, this **architectural landmark** (Дом Наркомфина; Novinsky bul 25; Ⓜ Barrikadnaya) was an early experiment in semi-communal living. Designed and built in the 1920s and in line with constructivist ideals, the communal space is maximised and individual space is minimised. Having been in a semi-ruinous state for many years, Narkomfin is finally undergoing restoration beginning in late 2017.

❼ Official Moscow

The **White House** (Белый дом; Krasnopresnenskaya nab 2; Ⓜ Krasnopresnenskaya) fronts a stately bend in the Moscow River, just north of the Novoarbatsky most. It was here that Boris Yeltsin rallied the opposition that confounded the 1991 hard-line coup, then two years later sent in tanks and troops to blast out conservative rivals.

❽ Commercial Moscow

In the distance, the **International Business Centre** (Москва-сити; Ⓜ Delovoi Tsentr) sprouts up along the Moscow River. Note the double-pronged City of Capitals building, representing Moscow and St Petersburg. The tallest building in Europe, the eastern spire of the Federation Tower, looms some 374m above the city.

❾ Post-Industrial Moscow

Tryokhgornaya Manufaktura (Трёхгорная Мануфактур; www.trekhgorka.ru; Rochdelskaya ul 15; ⊙9.30am-8.30pm Mon-Sat, 10am-6pm Sun; Ⓜ Barrikadnaya) is a former textile factory that has been converted into a hipster hub for eating, entertainment and design, so finish your tour at one of the many restaurants, bars and cafes on-site.

N

0 500 m
0 0.25 miles

For reviews see

⊙ Top Sights	p38
⊙ Sights	p44
⊗ Eating	p46
⊗ Drinking	p49
⊕ Entertainment	p51
⊞ Shopping	p52

Olympic Stadium & Sports Complex

per Vypolzov

Meshchanskaya ul

ul Durova

Lavrsky per

Olimpiysky pr

ul Sovetskoy Armii

Olimpiysky pr

Central Museum of the Armed Forces ⊙ 6

Frunze Central Army Park

ul Durova

Samotechnaya pl

Sadovaya-Sukharevskaya ul

ul Samotechnaya

Suvorovskaya pl

3-y Samotechny per

Gulag History Museum ⊙ 7

Delegatskaya ul

Institutny per

ul Dostoevskogo

Seleznevskaya ul

1-y Samotechny per

Jewish Museum & Centre of Tolerance ⊙ 5

ul Obraztsova

Novosushchyovskaya ul

Krasnoproletarskaya ul

Sadovaya-

Tikhvinskaya ul

Novoslobodskaya ul

Dolgorukovskaya ul

ul Palikha

Mendeleevskaya

Mendeleevskaya Ⓜ

Novoslobodskaya Ⓜ

ul Fadeeva

⊗ 23

Novoslobodskaya Ⓜ

Novoslobodskaya Ⓜ

ul Chayanova

Novolesnaya ul

Lesnaya ul

Mendeleevskaya Ⓜ

Miussky per

Miusskaya pl

ul Aleksandra Nevskogo

3-ya Tverskaya-Yamskaya ul

A **B** **C** **D** **E**

1 **2** **3** **4**

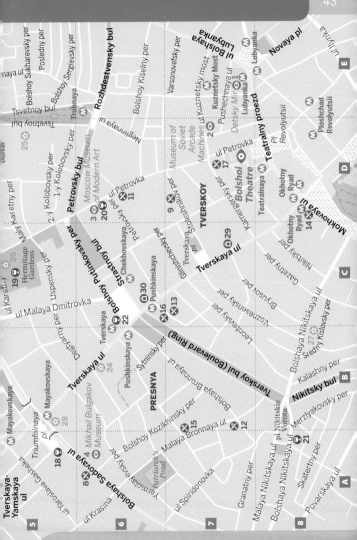

Sights

Detsky Mir
HISTORIC BUILDING

1 Map p42, E7

Dominated by the infamous KGB compound, Lubyanskaya ploshchad made adults shiver in Soviet times, but children dreamed of coming here, because another stately edifice in the square was filled with toys and goods intended entirely for them. Although the 1950s interior was lost in a 2008 reconstruction, it's worth visiting this children's department store to check out Soviet toy fashions at the Museum of Childhood and admire sweeping views of central Moscow from a rooftop observation point above it. (☎495-777 8077; www. detmir.ru; Teatralny pr 5/1; admission free; ⏱10am-10pm;)

Museum of Soviet Arcade Machines
MUSEUM

2 Map p42, D7

Growing up in the 1980s USSR was a peculiar, but not necessarily entirely bleak experience. Here is an example – a collection containing dozens of mostly functional Soviet arcade machines. At the entrance, visitors get a paper bag full of 15-kopek Soviet coins, which fire up these recreational dinosaurs that would look at home in the oldest episodes of Star Trek. (☎495-628 4515; http://15kop.ru; ul Kuznetsky most 12; admission incl tour ₽450; ⏱11am-9pm; Ⓜ Kuznetsky Most)

Moscow Museum of Modern Art
MUSEUM

3 Map p42, D6

A pet project of the ubiquitous artist Zurab Tsereteli, this museum is housed in a classical 18th-century merchant's home, originally designed by Matvei Kazakov (architect of the Kremlin Senate). It is the perfect light-filled setting for an impressive collection of 20th-century paintings, sculptures and graphics, which include both Russian and foreign artists. The highlight is the collection of avant-garde art, with works by Chagall, Kandinsky and Malevich. (Московский музей современного искусства; MMOMA; www.mmoma.ru; ul Petrovka 25; adult/student ₽450/250, joint ticket for three venues ₽500/300; ⏱noon-8pm Tue, Wed & Fri-Sun, 1-9pm Thu; Ⓜ Chekhovskaya)

Mikhail Bulgakov Museum
MUSEUM

4 Map p42, A6

Author of *The Master and Margarita* and *Heart of a Dog,* Mikhail Bulgakov was a Soviet-era novelist who was labelled a counter-revolutionary and was censored throughout his life. His most celebrated novels were published posthumously, earning him a sort of cult following in the late Soviet period. Bulgakov lived with his wife, Tatyana Lappa, in a flat in this block, which now houses an **arts centre and theatre** (Булгаковский Дом и Театр; www.dombulgakova.ru; ⏱1-11pm,

Detsky Mir

to 1am Fri & Sat) on the ground floor, and a small museum in their actual flat. (Музей Михаила Булгакова; www. bulgakovmuseum.ru; Bolshaya Sadovaya ul 10; adult/child ₽150/50; ⊘noon-7pm Tue-Sun, 2-9pm Thu; Ⓜ Mayakovskaya)

Jewish Museum & Centre of Tolerance   MUSEUM

5 ◉ Map p42, C1

Occupying a heritage garage, purpose-built to house a fleet of Leyland double-deckers that plied Moscow's streets in the 1920s, this vast museum, filled with cutting-edge multimedia technology, tackles the uneasy subject of relations between Jews and the Russian state over the centuries.

The exhibition relates the stories of pogroms, Jewish revolutionaries, the Holocaust and Soviet anti-Semitism in a calm and balanced manner. The somewhat limited collection of material exhibits is compensated for by the abundance of interactive video displays. (Еврейский музей и Центр толерантности; ☎495-645 0550; www. jewish-museum.ru; ul Obraztsova 11 str 1A; adult/student ₽400/200; ⊘noon-10pm Sun-Thu, 10am-3pm Fri; Ⓜ Novoslobodskaya)

Central Museum of the Armed Forces   MUSEUM

6 ◉ Map p42, D2

Covering the history of the Soviet and Russian military since 1917, this

Local Life

Hermitage Gardens

All the things that have improved Moscow parks no end in recent years now fill the small, charming **Hermitage Gardens** (Map p42, C5; Сады Эрмитажа; www.mosgorsad.ru; ul Karetny Ryad 3; admission free; ⊘24hr; MPushkinskaya) to the brim. Today, it is possibly the most happening place in Moscow, where art, food and crafts festivals, and concerts, occur almost weekly, especially in summer. Apart from the welcoming lawns and benches, it boasts a large children's playground, a summer cinema and a cluster of food and crafts kiosks. Come here to unwind and mingle with the coolest Muscovites.

massive museum occupies 24 halls plus open-air exhibits. Over 800,000 military items, including uniforms, medals and weapons, are on display. Among the highlights are remainders of the American U2 spy plane (brought down in the Ural Mountains in 1960) and the victory flag raised over Berlin's Reichstag in 1945. (Центральный музей Вооружённых Сил; ☎495-681 6303; www.cmaf.ru; ul Sovetskoy Armii 2; adult/student ₽200/100; ⊘10am-4.30pm Wed-Fri & Sun, to 6.30pm Sat; MDostoyevskaya)

Gulag History Museum   MUSEUM

7 ◉ Map p42, D3

Stalin's genocide is a subject many Russians prefer to forget rather than reflect on, but this modern multimedia space serves as both a learning centre and a memorial to the millions who perished in concentration camps for 'enemies of the people'. The centrepiece display of objects handmade by prisoners is especially moving. (Музей истории ГУЛАГа; ☎495-621 7310; www.gmig.ru; 1-y Samotechny per 9 str 1; adult/student ₽300/150; ⊘11am-6pm Tue, Wed & Fri, noon-8pm Thu; MDostoyevskaya)

Eating

Stolle   CAFE $

8 Map p42, A6

The entire menu at Stolle is excellent, but the *pirozhki* (savoury pies) are irresistible. A 'stolle' is a traditional Saxon Christmas cake: the selection of sweets and savouries sits on the counter, fresh from the oven. It may be difficult to decide (mushroom or meat, apricot or apple?), but you really can't go wrong. (Штолле; www.stolle.ru; Bldg 1, Bolshaya Sadovaya ul 3; mains ₽200-400; ⊘8am-11pm; ❄🛜👶; MMayakovskaya)

Lepim i Varim   RUSSIAN $

9 Map p42, D7

This cosy place touts itself as 'the most visited boutique' in the flashy Stoleshnikov per, but instead of Armani clothes it celebrates arguably the most vital item on any Russian menu – *pelmeni* (dumplings), as well as their relatives from all around the world. Perfectly shaped, the dumplings seem fit for a catwalk display in Milan and taste even better. (Лепим и варим; ☑8-985-688 9606; www. lepimivarim.ru; Stoleshnikov per 9, str 1; mains ₽220-350; ⓒ10am-11pm)

Delicatessen INTERNATIONAL $$

10 Map p42, C4

The affable and chatty owners of this place travel the world and experiment with the menu a lot, turning burgers, pizzas and pasta into artfully constructed objects of modern culinary art. The other source of joy is a cabinet filled with bottles of ripening fruity liquors, which may destroy your budget if consumed uncontrollably (a pointless warning, we know). (Деликатесы; www. newdeli.ru; Sadovaya-Karetnaya ul 20; mains ₽500-800; ⓒnoon-midnight Tue-Sun; 🛜; Ⓜ Tsvetnoy Bulvar)

Lavka-Lavka INTERNATIONAL $$

11 Map p42, D6

Welcome to the Russian Portlandia – all the food here is organic and hails from little farms where you may rest assured all the lambs and chickens lived a very happy life before being served to you on a plate. Irony aside, this is a great place to sample local food cooked in a funky improvisational style. (Лавка-Лавка; ☑8-903-115 5033; www.restoran.lavkalavka. com; ul Petrovka 21, str 2; mains ₽500-950; ⓒnoon-midnight Tue-Thu & Sun, to 1am Fri & Sat; 🛜🚸; Ⓜ Teatralnaya)

Twins RUSSIAN $$

12 Map p42, B7

Swoon-worthy identical-twin chefs Sergei and Ivan Berezutskiy bring their contrasting tastes and creative talents to this delightful restaurant. The brothers take a thoroughly modern approach to Russian cooking, with ingredients procured from all corners of the country. Seating is on the pleasant terrace or in the classy, kitschy dining room. (☑495-695 4510; www.twinsmoscow.ru; Malaya Bronnaya ul 13; mains ₽650-1750; 🛜🚹; Ⓜ Tverskaya)

Khachapuri GEORGIAN $$

13 Map p42, C7

Unassuming, affordable and appetising, this urban cafe exemplifies what people love about Georgian culture: the warm hospitality and the freshly baked *khachapuri* (cheese bread). Aside from eight types of delicious *khachapuri,* there's also an array of soups, shashlyk (kebabs), *khinkali* (dumplings) and other Georgian favourites. (Хачапури; ☑8-985-764 3118; www.hacha.ru; Bolshoy Gnezdnikovsky per 10; khachapuri ₽220-420, mains ₽430-690; ❄🛜; Ⓜ Pushkinskaya)

Gran Cafe Dr Zhivago RUSSIAN $$

14 Map p42, D8

An excellent breakfast choice before visiting the Kremlin, this round-the-clock place mixes Soviet nostalgia with a great deal of mischievous irony in both design and food. The chef has upgraded the menu of a standard pioneer camp's canteen to near-haute-cuisine level, with masterfully cooked porridge, pancakes, *vareniki* (dumplings) and cottage-cheese pies. (Гранд Кафе Dr Живаго; ☑ 499-922 0100; www.drzhivago.ru; Mokhovaya ul 15/1; mains ₽540-1200; ☉24hr; Ⓜ Okhotny Ryad)

Mari Vanna RUSSIAN $$

 15 Map p42, B7

Ring the doorbell at No 10 and you'll be ushered into the homey environs. Inside, the shelves are stuffed with books, photographs and mismatched tea sets, and old Soviet programs are showing on the black-and-white TV. Here you'll be served delicious Russian home cooking on little plates. You

Top Tip
Pushkin Konditerskaya

If you want to impress your date, but you can't afford the Cafe Pushkin for dinner, head next door to the confectionary shop **Pushkin Konditerskaya** (Кондитерская "Кафе ПушкинЪ."; www.sweetpushkin.ru; Tverskoy bul 26; candies ₽75-175, desserts from ₽400; ☉10am-11pm; 雨; ⓂPushkinskaya) for dessert. It's every bit as opulent as the restaurant, from the chandeliers down to the marble floors, with plenty of embellishments in between (not the least of which is the glass case displaying the sweets).

may even get a visit from the friendly resident *kiska* (pussy cat). (Мари Vanna; ☑ 495-650 6500; www.marivanna.ru; Spiridonyevsky per 10; mains ₽600-900; ☉9am-midnight; ☑ 雨; ⓂPushkinskaya)

Cafe Pushkin RUSSIAN $$$

 16 Map p42, C6

The tsarina of *haute-russe* dining, offering an exquisite blend of Russian and French cuisines. Service and food are done to perfection. The lovely 19th-century building has a different atmosphere on each floor, including a richly decorated library and a pleasant rooftop cafe. (Кафе ПушкинЪ; ☑ 495-739 0033; www.cafe-pushkin.ru; Tverskoy bul 26a; business lunch ₽620-930, mains ₽1000-2500; ☉24hr; ❄ 🛜; ⓂPushkinskaya)

Brasserie Most FRENCH $$$

17 Map p42, D7

Moscow's most venerated and erudite restaurateur Aleksander Rappoport shares his love for regional French cuisine in this classy and expensive place on Kuznetsky most. The menu is a grand gastrotour taking in seemingly every major area of France from Brittany to Alsace. Authenticity is religion here. If they say bouillabaisse, you can be sure it will taste exactly like Marseille's best. (☑ 495-660 0706; www.brasseriemost.ru; ul Kuznetsky most 6/3; mains ₽1000-3000; ☉8am-midnight Mon-Fri, from 9am Sat & Sun; ⓂTeatralnaya)

Cafe Pushkin

Drinking

Noor / Electro
BAR

There is little to say about this misleadingly unassuming bar (see 24 ⭐ Map p42, B6) , apart from the fact that everything in it is close to perfection. It has it all – prime location, convivial atmosphere, eclectic DJ music, friendly bartenders and superb drinks. Though declared 'the best' by various magazines on several occasions, it doesn't feel like they care. (📞8-903-136 7686; www.noorbar.com; ul Tverskaya 23/12; 🕐8pm-3am Mon-Wed, to 6am Thu-Sun; Ⓜ Pushkinskaya)

Time-Out Rooftop Bar
COCKTAIL BAR

18 Ⓠ Map p42, A5

On the upper floors of the throwback **Peking Hotel** (Гостиница Пекин; 📞495-650 0900; www.hotelpeking.ru; Bolshaya Sadovaya ul 5/1), this trendy bar is nothing but 'now'. That includes the bartenders sporting plaid and their delicious concoctions, specially created for different times of the day. The decor is pretty impressive – particularly the spectacular city skyline view. A perfect place for sundowners (or sun-ups, if you last that long). (http://hotelpeking.ru/timeout-rooftop-bar; 12th fl, 🕐noon-2am Sun-Thu, to 6am Fri & Sat; Ⓜ Mayakovskaya)

Understand

Flacon & Khlebozavod 9

Like the Bolsheviks a hundred years ago, Moscow hipsters are capturing one factory after another and redeveloping them, according to their tastes. **Flacon** (www.flacon.ru; ul Bolshaya Novodmitrovskaya 36; [M]Dmitrovskaya) is a mixture of brightly painted buildings and bare red brick resembling Portobello Rd in London. Once a glassware plant that produced bottles for the perfume industry, it is now home to dozens of funky shops and other businesses. Shopping for designer clothes and unusual souvenirs is the main reason for coming here.

The main shopping area covers three floors of the factory's central building. Climb to the top to find **Zaporozhets Heritage** ([☎]925-465 3410; http://zaporojec.ru; ul Bolshaya Novodmitrovskaya 36; [◷]11am-9pm; [M]Dmitrovskaya) – a shop representing a brand that produces clothes themed on classic Soviet children's cartoons. You'll also find several cool cafes, a cinema and even a summertime swimming pool in the area.

Nearby, **Khlebozavod 9** is a former bread factory that was was filling up with bars and boutiques at the time of writing. The front entrance is across the road from Flacon.

32.05
CAFE

19 🚇 Map p42, C5

The biggest drinking and eating establishment in Hermitage Gardens, this verandah positioned at the back of the park's main building looks a bit like a greenhouse. In summer, tables (and patrons) spill out into the park, making it one of the city's best places for outdoor drinking. With its long bar and joyful atmosphere, the place also heaves in winter. ([☎]905-703 3205; www.veranda3205.ru; ul Karetny Ryad 3; [◷]11am-3am; [M]Pushkinskaya)

Cafe Mart
CAFE

20 🚇 Map p42, D6

It looks like just another cellar bar, but if you walk all the way through the underground maze you'll find yourself in the huge overground 'orangerie' hall with mosaic-covered walls, warm lighting and possibly a jazz concert. When the weather is fine, Mart spills into the sculpture-filled courtyard of the adjacent Moscow Museum of Contemporary Art. (Кафе Март; www.cafemart.ru; ul Petrovka 25; [◷]11am-midnight Sun-Wed, 11am-6am Thu-Sat, jazz concert 9pm Thu; [♿]; [M]Chekhovskaya)

Art Lebedev Cafe Studio
CAFE

21 Map p42, A8

Owned by design guru Artemy Lebedev, this tiny space invites an attractive arty crowd to sip fancy coffee drinks and exotic teas. Regulars love the house-made *kasha* (porridge) for breakfast and the shady terrace in summer months. Don't miss the shop downstairs. (Кафе Студия Артемия Лебедева; www.artlebedev.ru; Bolshaya Nikitskaya ul 35b; ⏱8am-11pm Mon-Fri, from 10am Sat & Sun; 🛜; MАrbatskaya)

Glavpivmag
CRAFT BEER

22 🍺 Map p42, C6

Strategically located on the city's busiest square, this place has nothing but a long bar and lots of taps pumping from barrels, representing dozens of microbreweries from all over Russia and its near vicinity. This is Moscow's craft-beer central. The brew can be consumed on the spot or poured into takeaway bottles. (Главпивмаг; ☎8-965-223 4492; http://glavpivmag.com; Tverskaya ul 18; ⏱10am-3am; MТverskaya)

Svoboda
BAR

23 🍺 Map p42, B2

A flagship of the new converted factory space, Khlebozavod 9, this is a relatively large two-level bar specialising in craft beer. At the end of the week, local bands play live gigs on the stage shaped like a rollerblading ramp. Food is served, too. (Novodmitrovskaya ul 1, str 9; ⏱noon-11.30pm; MDmitrovskaya)

Entertainment

Stanislavsky Electrotheatre
ARTS CENTRE

24 ⭐ Map p42, B6

Renowned performance artist Boris Yukhananov has revived this old theatre as Moscow's hottest venue for experimental performance and visual art. Dance, music, cinema and theatre form a sparkling cocktail of genres and there is not a day without something new, strange and exciting going on. (☎495-699 7224; http://electrotheatre.ru; ul Tverskaya 23; MPushkinskaya)

Nikulin Circus on Tsvetnoy Bulvar
CIRCUS

25 ⭐ Map p42, D5

Founded in 1880, this circus is now named after beloved actor and clown Yury Nikulin (1921–97), who performed at the studio here for many years. Nikulin's shows centre on a given theme, which serves to add some cohesion to the productions. There are lots of trapeze artists, tightrope walkers and performing animals. (Цирк Никулина на Цветном бульваре; ☎495-625 8970; www.circusnikulin.ru; Tsvetnoy bul 13; tickets ₽400-2500; ⏱box office 11am-2pm & 3-7pm; MTsvetnoy Bulvar)

Novaya Opera
OPERA

26 ⭐ Map p42, C5

This theatre company was founded in 1991 by then-mayor Luzhkov and

Local Life

Local Fashion

Moscow designers are hard at work, fusing contemporary international styles with elements that are uniquely Russian. Find innovative duds by local designers at **Roomchik** (Map p42, D7; ☏495-629 6241; http://roomchik.ru; ul Bolshaya Dmitrovka 9, entrance 2, fl 2; ◷noon-9pm) or at **ADRESS** (Map p42, C8; Адрес; www.adresscollection.ru; Bolshoy Kislovskiy per 4; ◷10am-9pm Mon-Sat, to 8pm Sun; ⓂArbatskaya). Another name to know is **Katya Dobryakova** (Map p42, B6; www.katyadobryakova.com; Bolshoy Palashev per 1; ◷11am-10pm; ⓂTverskaya).

artistic director Evgeny Kolobov. Maestro Kolobov stated, 'we do not pretend to be innovators in this beautiful and complicated genre of opera'. As such, the 'New Opera' stages the old classics, and does it well. The gorgeous, modern opera house is set amid the Hermitage Gardens. (Новая опера; ☏495-694 0868; www.novayaopera.ru; ul Karetny Ryad 3; ◷box office noon-7.30pm; ⓂTsvetnoy Bulvar)

Moscow Tchaikovsky Conservatory
CLASSICAL MUSIC

27 ⭐ Map p42, B8

The country's largest music school, named for Tchaikovsky of course, has two venues, both of which host concerts, recitals and competitions. The Great Hall of the Conservatory is home to the Moscow Symphony Orchestra (MSO; www.moscowsymphony.ru), a low-budget but highly lauded orchestra under the direction of Vladimir Ziva. (Московская консерватория имени Чайковского; ☏box office 495-629 9401; www.mosconsv.ru; Bolshaya Nikitskaya ul 13; ⓂOkhotny Ryad)

Tchaikovsky Concert Hall
CLASSICAL MUSIC

28 ⭐ Map p42, B5

Home to the famous Moscow State Philharmonic (Moskovskaya Filharmonia), the capital's oldest symphony orchestra, Tchaikovsky Concert Hall was established in 1921. It's a huge auditorium, with seating for 1600 people. Expect to hear the Russian classics such as Stravinsky, Rachmaninov and Shostakovich, as well as other European favourites. Look out for children's concerts, jazz ensembles and other special performances. (Концертный зал имени Чайковского; ☏495-232 0400; www.meloman.ru; Triumfalnaya pl 4/31; tickets ₽800-3000; ◷concerts 7pm, closed Aug; ⓂMayakovskaya)

Shopping

Transylvania
MUSIC

29 🔒 Map p42, C7

From the courtyard, look for the black metal door that leads down into this dungeon of a shop, which houses room after room of CDs, in

Performers, Nikulin Circus on Tsvetnoy Bulva (p51)

every genre imaginable. If you are curious about the *russky* rock scene, this is where you can sample some songs. (☎495-629 8786; www.transylvania.ru; Tverskaya ul 6/1, bldg 5; ⊙11am-10pm; Ⓜ Teatralnaya)

Yeliseev Grocery   FOOD & DRINKS

30 🔒 Map p42, C6

Peek in here for a glimpse of pre-revolutionary grandeur, as the store is set in the former mansion of the successful merchant Yeliseev. It now houses an upscale market selling caviar and other delicacies. It's a great place to shop for souvenirs for your foodie friends back home. (Елисеевский магазин; Tverskaya ul 14; ⊙8am-9pm Mon-Sat, 10am-6pm Sun; Ⓜ Pushkinskaya)

Explore

Arbat, Khamovniki & Zamoskvorechie

These districts south of the city are rich with culture. Moscow's most famous street, ul Arbat, is something of an art market, while the nearby streets are lined with museums and galleries. Across the river, Zamoskvorechie is unique for its low-rise buildings, quaint court-yards and onion domes. These enticing neighbourhoods are home to celebrated art museums, a historic monastery and a beloved city park.

The Sights in a Day

 Dedicate your morning to browsing the impressive exhibit at the **Pushkin Museum of Fine Arts** (p56) and/or one of the smaller galleries in the area. Have a meat-lover's lunch at **Voronezh** (p68).

Take a peak inside the **Cathedral of Christ the Saviour** (p64) while you're in the neighbourhood. Then stroll across the pedestrian bridge and continue along the Krymskaya nab, stopping to play in the fountains and admire the eclectic collection of sculptures at **Art Muzeon** (p64). Spend the rest of your afternoon at **Gorky Park** (pictured left; p58) – cycling, strolling, sunbathing etc. Pop into **Garage Museum of Contemporary Art** (p59) to see Moscow's most cutting-edge art museum.

The best place to experience modern Moscow nightlife is at **Red October** (p64) – a former chocolate factory that is now an island of post-industrial cool, packed with restaurants, bars, galleries and shops. Whether you're dining or drinking (or both) you'll have many venues to choose from.

For a local's day in Arbat, see p60.

Top Sights

Pushkin Museum of Fine Arts (p56)

Gorky Park (p58)

Local Life

Along the Stary Arbat (p60)

♥ Best of Arbat, Khamovniki & Zamoskvorechie

Museums & Galleries
Pushkin Museum of Fine Arts (p56)

State Tretyakov Gallery (p64)

Garage Museum of Contemporary Art (p59)

Getting There

Ⓜ **Metro** The dark-blue and light-blue lines run in parallel across the Arbat district. They have eponymous but unconnected stations at Arbatskaya and Smolenskaya.

Ⓜ **Metro** Line 1 (red) traverses the Khamovniki district, with stops at Kropotkinskaya, Park Kultury and Sportivnaya.

Ⓜ **Metro** Three different metro lines cut through Zamoskvorechie in a north–south direction. Most useful, the orange and green lines intersect at Novokuznetskaya.

Top Sights
Pushkin Museum of Fine Arts

This is Moscow's premier foreign-art museum, split over three branches and showing off a broad selection of European works, including masterpieces from ancient civilisations, the Italian Renaissance and the Dutch Golden Age, not to mention an incredible collection of Impressionist and post-Impressionist paintings in the 19th and 20th Century Art Gallery.

Музей изобразительных искусств им Пушкина

⊙ Map p62, C1

www.arts-museum.ru

ul Volkhonka 12

single/combined galleries ₽300/550

🕑11am-7pm Tue, Wed & Fri-Sun, to 9pm Thu

Ⓜ Kropotkinskaya

Main Building

The main building opened in 1912 as the museum of Moscow University. It now exhibits the bulk of the holdings that date from antiquity through the 18th century. The museum contains many masterpieces from the Italian Renaissance. Artists such as Botticelli, Tiepolo and Veronese are all represented. The highlight is perhaps the Dutch masterpieces from the Golden Age of Dutch art. The rest of Europe is also well represented. The Ancient Civilization exhibits contain a surprisingly excellent collection, complete with ancient Egyptian weaponry, jewellery, ritual items and tombstones.

19th & 20th Century Art Gallery

The separate **19th and 20th Century Art Gallery** (ul Volkhonka 14; adult/student ₽300/150; ⊙11am-7pm Tue-Sun, to 9pm Thu) contains a famed assemblage of Impressionist and post-Impressionist works, based on the collections of two well-known Moscow art patrons, Sergei Shchukin and Ivan Morozov. It includes paintings by Degas, Manet, Renoir and Pisarro, with an entire room dedicated to Monet.

Other highlights include Rodin's sculptures and many famous paintings by Matisse. There are also some lesser-known pieces by Van Gogh and Picasso; a few exquisite primitive paintings by Rousseau; and room devoted to Gaugin. The rich collection of 20th-century art continues to grow, with works by Miro, Kandinsky, Chagall and Arp.

Museum Town

In 2017, the Pushkin Museum of Fine Arts commenced a vast expansion and redesign known as 'Museum Town'. Exhibition space is expected to double and the surrounding neighbourhood will be transformed. The Museum Town project is supposed to be completed in 2019, after which the location of the exhibits may be changed.

☑ Top Tips

▶ A combination ticket (adult/student ₽550/300) includes admission to both the main building and the 19th and 20th Century Art Gallery

▶ Audio guides in English are available for the main building (₽350) and the 19th and 20th Century Art Gallery (₽300).

✄ Take a Break

Opposite the main building, Professor Puf (p67) is a convenient and pleasant option for breakfast, lunch or afternoon sweet.

Walk a few blocks to Voronezh (p68) for delicious sandwiches or meaty mains.

Top Sights
Gorky Park

Moscow's main city getaway is not your conventional expanse of nature preserved deep inside an urban jungle. Its mission is to mix leisure and culture in equal proportions. Designed in the 1920s by avant-garde architect Konstantin Melnikov as a piece of communist utopia, these days it showcases the enlightened transformation Moscow has undergone in recent years.

Парк Горького

👁 Map p62, C5

admission free

🕐 24hr

🚻

Ⓜ Oktyabrskaya

Activities

Activities include cycling, rollerblading, beach volleyball, urban and extreme sports, table tennis and even pétanque. There are several bicycle- and skate-rental places around the park, with one conveniently located under the Andreyevsky pedestrian bridge.

In summer, young people gather to salsa, swing dance or polka. The epicentre of this dance craze is located on the boardwalk under Andreyevsky Bridge, but there are a few more dancing venues inside the park.

In winter, the ponds are flooded, turning the park into the city's biggest ice-skating rink.

The list of activities on offer could easily cover the Rosetta Stone, although on sunny days thousands opt for complete inactivity atop one of the giant cushions scattered around the park.

Garage Museum of Contemporary Art

The brainchild of Moscow art fairy Darya Zhukova, **Garage** (☎495-645 0520; www.garagemca.org; ul Krymsky val 9/32; adult/student ₽400/200; ☺11am-10pm) is one of the capital's hottest modern-art venues. In mid-2015 the museum moved to spectacular new digs in Gorky Park – a derelict Soviet-era building, renovated by the visionary Dutch architect Rem Koolhaas. It hosts exhibitions, lectures, films and interactive educational programs, featuring Russian and international artists both here and at Garage Screen open-air cinema, located across the square.

As you enter, pay attention to the part-ruined, Soviet-era wall mosaics, conserved in the manner of ancient mosaics.

☑ **Top Tips**

▶ You can observe the park as well as much of Moscow from the top of the giant Stalin-era arch at the entrance. Access is via the Gorky Park Museum.

▶ The park is packed to the brim with revellers over weekends, when many concerts and other events take place.

▶ Come during the week if you need some rest from the city buzz.

✗ **Take a Break**

The whole place is designed for taking a break from work and urban madness! The park is dotted with eateries, such as AC/DC in Tbilisi (p67).

For drinks (and a game of pétanque) head to Le Boule (p70).

Local Life
Along the Stary Arbat

The 'old' Arbat is the historic haunt of artists, musicians and street performers. Though Arbat today has been taken over by souvenir stands and is often packed with tourists, it still evokes the free-thinking artistic spirit of yesteryear.

1 Moorish Castle

Studded with seashells, the House of **Friendship with Peoples of Foreign Countries** (Дом дружбы с народами зарубежных стран; Vozdvizhenka ul 16; MArbatskaya) was built in 1899 for an eccentric merchant, Arseny Morozov, who was inspired by a real Moorish castle in Spain. The inside (not open to the public) is sumptuous and equally over the top. Morozov's mother, who lived next door, appar-

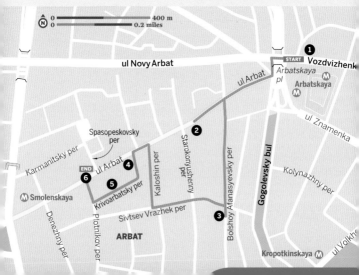

ently declared of her son's home, 'Until now, only I knew you were mad; now everyone will'.

② Art Market

Strolling up ul Arbat, sidewalk art and street performers stand beside souvenir stalls and costumed characters. There are many treasures on display (and for sale) at the **Association of Artists of the Decorative Arts** (Ассоциация художников декоративно-прикладного искусства; AHDI; www.ahdi.ru; ul Arbat 21; ⊙11am-8pm; Ⓜ Arbatskaya), where pottery, clothing and handicrafts make for unique souvenirs.

③ Sculptural Surpises

Look out for strange and beautiful sculptures dotting the yards and courtyards on Sivtsev Vrazhek per. They are the work of Alexander Burganov, whose nearby studio is filled with whimsical treasures. Part studio, part museum, the **Burganov House** (Дом Бурганова; ☏ 495-695 0429; www.burganov.ru; Bolshoy Afanasyevsky per 15; adult/child ₽150/100; ⊙11am-7pm Sat-Wed, noon-9pm Thu; Ⓜ Kropotkinskaya) is a unique venue in Moscow, where the craft goes on around you, as you peruse the sculptures and other artwork on display. Comprising several interconnected courtyards and houses, the works of the surrealist sculptor are artfully displayed alongside pieces from the artist's private collection.

④ Street Art

Get a glimpse of the counterculture of the old Arbat at the corner of Krivoarbatsky per and ul Arbat, where the Viktor Tsoy memorial wall is dedicated to the lead singer of the Soviet rock band Kino. Tsoy achieved cult-idol status in 1990 when he died in a car crash at a tragically young age.

⑤ Avant-garde Anamoly

The only private house built during the Soviet period, the **home of Konstantin Melnikov** (Дом Мельникова; ☏ 495-697 8037; Krivoarbatsky per 10; ⊙courtyard 10am-7pm Mar-Oct, to 5pm Nov-Feb, house by appointment; Ⓜ Arbatskaya) stands as testament to the innovation of the Russian avant-garde. The architect created his unusual home from two interlocking cylinders – an ingenious design that employs no internal load-bearing wall. It was also experimental in its designation of living space, as the whole family slept in one room, divided by narrow screens.

⑥ Bard of the Arbat

You can't miss the statue of Bulat Okudzhava, the beloved bard who lived and performed on this storied street. Okudzhava inspired a whole movement of liberal-thinking poets to take their ideas to the streets. The Arbat today, crowded with tacky souvenir shops and overpriced cafes, bears little resemblance to the hallowed haunt of Okudzhava's youth. But its memory lives on in the bards and buskers, painters and poets who still perform for strolling crowds on summer evenings.

A
B
C
D

1

2

3

4

5

Ⓜ Smolenskaya
ul Arbat
❌ 10
Novinsky bul
Ⓜ Smolenskaya
Sivtsev Vrazhek per
Denezhny per
Starokonyushenny per
Bolshoy Afanasyevsky per
Gogolevsky bul
▲ 26 🔒
18
ul Znamenka
Kolymazhny per
Borovitskaya
Ⓜ

Pushkin Museum of Fine Arts ◉
Bolsho
Kamen
most
❌ 12
ul Volkhonka

Gagarinsky per
Prechistensky per
Chisty per
ul Prechistenka
❌ 13
Kropotkinskaya Ⓜ
14 ❌ Ⓜ
Soymonovsky proezd
Cathedral of Christ the Saviour
1 ◉
Bolot
p
Bolotny Island

Smolensky bul
Bolshoy Levshinsky per
2-y Obydensky per
Pozharsky per
Prechistenskaya nab
🏛 19
Red October
3 ◉
❌ 9
23 🏛❌ 15
20 🏛

KHAMOVNIKI
Mansurovsky per
ul Ostozhenka
❌ 22
Korobeynikov per
Khilkov per
Kropotkinsky per
Smolensky bul
ul Timura Frunze
Bolshaya Pirogovskaya ul
◉ 7
8
Park Kultury Ⓜ
Park Kultury Ⓜ
Krymsky most
Krymskaya nab
Art Muzeon & Krymskaya Naberezhnaya ◉ 4
Yakimanskaya nab
1-y Golutvinsky
Prechistenskaya nab
ul Bolshaya Yakim

Tolstoy Estate-Museum ◉ 6
ul Lva Tolstogo
Obolensky per
Nesvizhsky per
Frunzenskaya nab
Krymsky most
5 ◉
New Tretyakov Gallery
Iskusstv Park
ul Krymsky val (Garden Ring)
Maronovsky per
Oktyabrs
ul Bolshaya Yakim

Moscow River
Gorky Park ◉
Pushkinskaya nab
21 🏛 ❌ 11
Garage Museum of Contemporary Art
Oktyabrskaya Ⓜ
Leninsky pr

For reviews see
◉ Top Sights   p56
◉ Sights   p64
❌ Eating   p66
🍷 Drinking   p70
⭐ Entertainment   p71
🔒 Shopping   p71

Ⓝ
0 _____ 500 m
0 _____ 0.25 miles

E

F

G

H

exander
arden

emlevskaya nab

Sofiyskaya nab

Bolshoy
Moskvoretsky
Most

Moskvoretskaya nab

Rauzhskaya nab

Ustinsky per

Serebryanicheskaya nab

Bernikovskaya nab

1

Yauzskaya ul

ul Goncharnaya

pinsky
kver
olotnaya nab
borvodny Canal.

Chugunny
most

Maly
Moskvoretsky
Most

Komissariatsky
most

2

Moscow River

Kotelnicheskaya nab

Lavrushinsky per

State
Tretyakov
Gallery
Main Branch

Pyatnitskaya ul

Runovsky per

Ⓧ**17**

24 Ⓜ **Novokuznetskaya**

Klimentovsky per
Ⓜ **Tretyakovskaya**

Sadovnicheskaya ul
Sadovnicheskaya nab
Ozerkovskaya nab

Ozerkovsky per

Kosmodamianskaya nab

Kosmodamianskaya nab

Ⓜ **Bolshaya
anka**

Polyanka
ul Bolshaya

ul Bolshaya Ordynka

Pyatnitskaya ul

Novokuznetskaya ul

1-y Novokuznetsky per

ul Bakhrushina

Tatarskaya ul

Nizhnyaya Krasnokholmskaya ul

Narodnaya ul

Krasnokholmskaya nab

3

Ⓩ
25

4

Paveletskaya Ⓜ

Kozhevnicheskaya ul

itnaya ul
obryninskaya Ⓜ

ul Valovaya   **Valovaya ul**

Ⓜ **Serpukhovskaya**

Paveletsky Ⓐ
Vokzal

Dubininskaya ul

Kozhevnicheskaya ul

Letnikovskaya ul

5

1-y Dobryninsky per

Ⓧ**16** ▼
Lyusinovskaya ul

Stremyanny per

Bolshaya Pionerskaya ul

Dubininskaya ul

Sights

Cathedral of Christ the Saviour

CHURCH

1 ◎ Map p62, C2

This gargantuan cathedral was completed in 1997 – just in time to celebrate Moscow's 850th birthday. It is amazingly opulent, garishly grandiose and truly historic. The cathedral's sheer size and splendour guarantee its role as a love-it-or-hate-it landmark. Considering Stalin's plan for this site (a Palace of Soviets topped with a 100m statue of Lenin), Muscovites should at least be grateful they can admire the shiny domes of a church instead of the shiny dome of Ilyich's head. (Храм Христа Спасителя; www.xxc.ru; ul Volkhonka 15; admission free; ⊙1-5pm Mon, from 10am Tue-Sun; MKropotkinskaya)

State Tretyakov Gallery Main Branch

GALLERY

2 ◎ Map p62, E2

The exotic boyar castle on a little lane in Zamoskvorechie contains the main branch of the State Tretyakov Gallery, housing the world's best collection of Russian icons and an outstanding collection of other pre-revolutionary Russian art. Show up early to beat the queues. The neighbouring **Engineer's Building** is reserved for special exhibits. (Главный отдел Государственной Третьяковской галереи; www.tretyakovgallery.ru; Lavrushin-sky per 10; adult/child ₽500/200; ⊙10am-6pm Tue, Wed & Sun, to 9pm Thu-Sat, last tickets 1hr before closing; MTretyakovskaya)

Red October

ARTS CENTRE

3 ◎ Map p62, D2

This defiant island of Russian modernity and European-ness is a vibrant arts centre filled with cool bars, restaurants and galleries. With an aptly revolutionary name, the former Red October chocolate factory looks straight into the Kremlin's eyes – a vivid reminder that Russia is not all about totalitarian control and persecution. (Завод Красный Октябрь; Bersenevskaya nab; admission free; MKropotkinskaya)

Art Muzeon & Krymskaya Naberezhnaya

PUBLIC ART

4 ◎ Map p62, D3

Moscow's answer to London's South Bank, Krymskaya Naberezhnaya (Crimea Embankment) features wave-shaped street architecture with Scandinavian-style wooden elements, beautiful flower beds and a moody fountain, which ejects water randomly from many holes in the ground to the excitement of children and adults alike. It has merged with the Art Muzeon park and its motley collection of Soviet stone idols (Stalin, Sverdlov, a selection of Lenins and Brezhnevs) that were ripped from their pedestals in the post-1991 wave of anti-Soviet feeling. (admission free; MPark Kultury)

Cathedral of Christ the Saviour

New Tretyakov Gallery

GALLERY

5 ⊙ Map p62, C3

Moscow's premier venue for 20th-century Russian art, this branch of the State Tretyakov Gallery has much more than the typical socialist-realist images of muscle-bound men wielding scythes and busty women milking cows (although there's that, too). The exhibits showcase avant-garde artists such as Malevich, Kandinsky, Chagall, Goncharova and Popova, as well as non-conformist artists of the 1960s and 1970s who refused to accept the official style. Новая Третьяковская галерея; www.tretyakovgallery.ru; ul Krymsky val 10; adult/child ₽500/200; ⊙10am-6pm Tue, Wed & Sun, to 9pm Thu-Sat, last tickets 1hr before closing; M Park Kultury)

Tolstoy Estate-Museum

MUSEUM

6 ⊙ Map p62, A4

Leo Tolstoy's winter home during the 1880s and 1890s now houses an interesting museum dedicated to the writer's home life. While it's not particularly opulent or large, the building is fitting for junior nobility – which Tolstoy was. Exhibits here demonstrate how Tolstoy lived, as opposed to his literary influences, which are explored at the **Tolstoy Literary Museum** (Литературный музей Толстого; ul Prechistenka 11; adult/student ₽250/100;

> ### Understand
> ## Cathedral Past & Present
>
> The Cathedral of Christ the Saviour sits on the site of an earlier and similar church of the same name, built in the 19th century to commemorate Russia's victory over Napoleon. The original was destroyed in 1931, during Stalin's orgy of explosive secularism. His plan to replace the church with a 315m-high Palace of Soviets never got off the ground – literally. Instead, for 50 years the site served another important purpose: the world's largest swimming pool.

◎noon-6pm Tue-Sun; Ⓜ Kropotkinskaya). See the salon where Sergei Rachmaninov and Nikolai Rimsky-Korsakov played piano, and the study where Tolstoy himself wove his epic tales. (Музей-усадьба Толстого 'Хамовники'; www.tolstoymuseum.ru; ul Lva Tolstogo 21; adult/student ₽400/200; ◎10am-6pm Tue, Wed & Fri-Sun, noon-8pm Thu; Ⓜ Park Kultury)

Novodevichy Convent CONVENT

 7 ◎ Map p62, A3

The Novodevichy Convent was founded in 1524 to celebrate the taking of Smolensk from Lithuania, an important step in Moscow's conquest of the old Kyivan Rus lands. The oldest and most dominant building on the grounds is the white Smolensk Cathedral, with a sumptuous interior covered in 16th-century frescoes. Novodevichy is a functioning monastery. Women are advised to cover their heads and shoulders when entering the churches, while men should wear long pants. (Новодевичий монастырь; Novodevichy pr 1; adult/student ₽500/250, photos ₽300; ◎grounds 8am-8pm, museums 9am-5pm Wed-Mon; Ⓜ Sportivnaya)

Novodevichy Cemetery CEMETERY

 8 ◎ Map p62, A3

Adjacent to the Novodevichy Convent (p66), the Novodevichy Cemetery is one of Moscow's most prestigious resting places – a veritable who's who of Russian politics and culture. Here you will find the tombs of Bulgakov, Chekhov, Gogol, Mayakovsky, Prokofiev, Stanislavsky and Eisenstein among many other Russian and Soviet cultural luminaries. The most recent notable addition to the cemetery is former President Boris Yeltsin, whose tomb is marked by an enormous Russian flag. (Новодевичье кладбище; Luzhnetsky pr 2; admission free; ◎9am-5pm Ⓜ Sportivnaya)

Eating

Mizandari GEORGIAN $

9 ✕ Map p62, D2

Georgian restaurants in Moscow tend to be either expensive or tacky. This small family-run place is neither. Come with friends and order a selection of appetizers, such as *pkhali* and *lobio* (both made of walnut paste), *khachapuri* (cheese pastry) and *kharcho* (spicy lamb soup). Bless you if you can still accommodate a main course after all that! (☎8-903-263 9990; www.mizandari.ru; Bolotnaya nab 5, str 1; mains ₽300-500; ☺11am-11pm Sun-Thu, to midnight Fri & Sat; MKropotkinskaya)

Varenichnaya No 1   RUSSIAN $

10 Map p62, B1

Retro Soviet is all the rage in Moscow, and this old-style restaurant does it right, with books lining the walls, old movies on the B&W TV, and Cold War–era prices. The menu features tasty, filling *vareniki* and *pelmeni* (different kinds of dumplings), with sweet and savoury fillings. Bonus: an excellent house-made pickled vegie plate to make you pucker. (www.varenichnaya.ru; ul Arbat 29; business lunch ₽290-340, mains ₽220-490; ☺10am-midnight; ☑; MArbatskaya)

AC/DC in Tbilisi   GEORGIAN $

11 Map p62, C5

Burgers and Georgia (the one in the Caucasus) seem to inhabit parallel universes, but they get together in this summer-only Gorky Park kiosk. An otherwise very ordinary burger turns Georgian with the help of hot *adjika* sauce and *suluguni* cheese. The meatballs in walnut *satsivi* sauce are another thing to try here. (☎8-909-955 4043; www.facebook.com/acdcintbilisi; Gorky Park; mains ₽250-350; ☺10am-10pm; MOktyabrskaya)

Professor Puf   RUSSIAN $

12 Map p62, D1

A select menu of Russian classics shows off fresh ingredients, old-fashioned cooking methods and contemporary flair. Pleasant, efficient service and a super-central location make this a great option before or after a morning at the museum. Unfortunately named, but otherwise quite delightful, especially the house-made bread and pastries. (www.professorpuf.ru; Bldg 1, ul Volkhonka 9; breakfast ₽150-200, lunch ₽350-500; ☺8am-10pm Mon-Fri, from 10am Sat & Sun; ☎☑; MKropotkinskaya)

Elardzhi   GEORGIAN $$

13 Map p62, B2

Moscow's Georgian restaurants are all very tasty, but this one is also tasteful. You'll be charmed from the moment you enter the courtyard, where live rabbits and lambs greet all comers. Sink into a sofa in the romantic dining room or on the light-filled porch; then feast on delicacies, such as the namesake dish, *elarji* (cornmeal with Sulguni cheese). (Эларджи; ☎495-627 7897; www.ginza.ru; Gagarinsky per 15a; mains ₽600-800; ☺noon-midnight; ☑; MKropotkinskaya)

Voronezh
STEAK $$

14 Map p62, C2

When Voronezh first opened, foodies couldn't stop talking about how a classy new restaurant in the capital was named after a provincial town. Bold move by esteemed chef Alexander Rapoport. The fact is that Voronezh (the restaurant) is a celebration of meat, and all of this meat comes from the owner's ranch in Voronezh (the city). (Воронеж; 495-695 0641; www.voronej.com; ul Prechistenka 4; sandwiches ₽250-750, mains from ₽580; 8am-midnight; ; Kropotkinskaya)

Syrovarnya
EASTERN EUROPEAN $$

15 Map p62, D3

Domestic cheese production is all the rage in Russia, which has banned cheese imports from the EU in retaliation for Western sanctions. This restaurant serves hearty, homey meals, most of which contain cheese produced right here – in a micro-creamery that you see first thing after coming inside. A shop selling top-quality cheese is also on the premises. (495-727 3880; www.novikovgroup.ru/restaurants/syrovarnya; Bersenevsky per 2, str 1; mains ₽400-700; noon-midnight Mon-Thu, 24hr Fri-Sun; Polyanka, Kropotkinskaya)

Fedya, dich!
FUSION $$

16 Map p62, E5

Let's take a walk on the wild side of the Moscow food scene. This place gets fresh supplies of fish and game from faraway corners of Siberia. Sea of Japan oysters and Arctic fish tartare are fresh and delicious despite crossing eight time zones to land on your table; so are wild-boar cutlets and deer steaks with forest berries. (Федя, дичь!; 8-916-747 0110; Mytnaya ul 74; mains ₽650-820; 11am-11pm; Tulskaya)

Björn
SCANDINAVIAN $$$

17 Map p62, F2

A neat cluster of fir trees on a busy street hides a Nordic gem that deserves a saga to glorify its many virtues. This is not an 'ethnic' restaurant, but a presentation of futuristic Scandinavian cuisine straight out of a science-fiction movie. From salads to desserts, every dish looks deceptively simple, visually perfect and 23rd century. (495-953 9059; http://bjorn.rest; Pyatnitskaya ul 3; mains ₽600-1200; Novokuznetskaya)

Chemodan
RUSSIAN $$$

18 Map p62, C1

A unique opportunity to sample Siberian cuisine (rare, that is, for those of us who don't frequent Siberia). The menu highlights game meat, regional seafood and wild fruits and berries (and pine cones). The dining room is decorated with old photos and antiques, creating a romantic atmosphere that any adventurer would be happy to return home to. Highly recommended. (Чемодан; 495-695 3819; www.chemodan-msk.ru; Gogolevsky bul 25; mains ₽900-1950; ; Kropotkinskaya)

Understand

Georgian Cuisine

In her book *The Georgian Feast*, writer Darra Goldstein describes the former Soviet republic of Georgia as 'a land blessed by Heaven's table scraps'. Short of Heaven itself, Moscow is the best place outside the Caucasus to sample this rich, spicy cuisine.

The fertile region – wedged between East and West – has long been the beneficiary and victim of merchants and raiders passing through. These influences are evident in Georgian cooking, which shows glimpses of Mediterranean and Middle Eastern flavours. But the truly Georgian elements – the differences – are what make this cuisine so delectable. Most meat and vegetable dishes use ground walnuts or walnut oil as an integral ingredient, yielding a distinctive, nutty flavour. Also characteristic of Georgian cuisine is the spice mixture *khmeli-suneli*, which combines coriander, garlic, chillies, pepper and savory with a saffron substitute made from dried marigold petals.

Georgian chefs love to prepare food over an open flame, and grilled meats are among the tastiest items on any Georgian menu. Herbs such as coriander, dill and parsley are often served fresh, with no preparation or sauce, as a palate-cleansing counterpoint to rich dishes. Grapes and pomegranates show up not only as desserts, but also as tart complements to roasted meats.

The most beloved item on the Georgian menu is undoubtedly *khachapuri*, a rich, cheesy bread that is made with circles of fresh dough cooked with sour, salty *suluguni* cheese. Sometimes it is topped with a raw egg in the crater.

Around Moscow, there are scores of Georgian restaurants in all price ranges. Sample this delicious food now: you may not have another chance until you get to Tbilisi.

Top Tip

Coffee Bean

One could claim that **Coffee Bean** (Map p62, F2; www.coffeebean.ru; Pyatnitskaya ul 5; ⊙8am-11pm; MTretyakovskaya) started the coffee craze in Moscow. While the original location on Tverskaya ul is no longer open, there are a few of these excellent, affordable cafes around town. Try their trademark Raf coffee, invented years ago by a customer and now spreading around the world, without anyone realising it comes from Russia.

Drinking

Bar Strelka
CAFE, CLUB

19 Map p62, D2

Located just below the Patriarshy most, the bar-restaurant at the **Strelka Institute** (www.strelkainstitute.ru; MKropotkinskaya, Polyanka) is the ideal starting point for an evening in the Red October (p64) complex. The rooftop terrace has unbeatable Moscow River views, but the interior is equally cool in a shabby-chic sort of way. The bar menu is excellent and there is usually somebody tinkling the ivories. (www.barstrelka.com; Bersenevskaya nab 14/5, bldg 5a; ⊙9am-midnight Mon-Thu, to 3am Fri, noon-3am Sat, noon-midnight Sun; 🛜; MKropotkinskaya)

Gipsy
CLUB, CAFE

20 Map p62, D3

Euphoria reigns in this postmodern nomad camp of a bar with its strategic rooftop position on Red October (p64). The decor is bright-coloured kitsch, which among other oddities means fake palm trees and toilet doors covered with artificial fur. The DJ and live-music repertoires are aptly eclectic. (www.bargipsy.ru; Bolotnaya nab 3/4; ⊙6pm-1am Sun-Thu, 2pm-6am Fri & Sat)

Le Boule
BAR

21 Map p62, C5

The goatee and moustache factor is high in this hipster-ridden verandah bar that comes with a dozen pétanque lanes. Grab a pitcher of sangria or a pint of cider and have a go at what is arguably the most alcohol-compatible sport. Live bands often play on the verandah in the early evening. (📞495-518 8412; Gorky Park; ⊙noon-midnight; 🛜; MOktyabrskaya)

Dom 12
WINE BAR

22 Map p62, B3

Eclectic and atmospheric, Dom 12 may be the perfect place to attend an event or chat with friends over a glass of wine. The cosy interior is enhanced by natural materials, comfy chairs and low lighting. Besides the excellent wine list, the place offers poetry nights, lectures, concerts and dancing. Delightful! (www.dom12cafe.ru; Mansurovsky per 12; ⊙noon-6am; MPark Kultury)

Dictatura Estetica BAR

23 🎤 Map p62, D3

Aesthetics indeed rule this stylish little bar, but its main appeal lies in the gin cocktails based on secret potions, which its mixologists produce out of anything that grows. We tried the nettle mix and it tasted great. They serve quality food with South Asian motifs. (☎495-991 9946; www.facebook. com/dictaturabar; Bersenevskaya nab 6, str 1; ⊙24hr; Ⓜ️Polyanka, Kropotkinskaya)

Underdog CRAFT BEER

24 🎤 Map p62, F2

This cosy little pub hidden away from the perpetually crowded Klimentovsky per has the melancholy of Edward Hopper paintings or a good road movie. The beer menu is an all-encompassing list of IPAs, APAs, lagers, krieks and whatnot – mostly produced at local microbreweries. Some Russian beers come with crazy names such as Shaman Has Three Hands. (Klimentovsky per 12, str 14; ⊙2pm-2am; Ⓜ️Tretyakovskaya)

Entertainment

Moscow International House of Music CLASSICAL MUSIC

25 ⭐ Map p62, H4

This graceful, modern glass building has three halls, including Svetlanov Hall, which holds the largest organ in Russia. Needless to say, organ concerts held here are impressive. This is the usual venue for performances by the **National Philharmonic of Russia** (Национальный филармонический оркестр России; ☎495-730 3778; www. nfor.ru), a privately financed, highly lauded, classical-music organisation. Founded in 1991, the symphony is directed and conducted by the esteemed Vladimir Spivakov. (☎495-730 1011; www.mmdm.ru; Kosmodemyanskaya nab 52/8; tickets ₽200-2000; Ⓜ️Paveletskaya)

Shopping

Dom Knigi BOOKS

26 🔒 Map p62, C1

Among the largest bookshops in Moscow, Dom Knigi has a selection of foreign-language books to rival any other shop in the city, not to mention travel guidebooks, maps, and reference and souvenir books. This huge, crowded place hosts regularly scheduled readings, children's programs and other bibliophilic activities. (Дом Книги; www.mdk-arbat.ru; ul Novy Arbat 8; ⊙9am-11pm Mon-Fri, from 10am Sat & Sun; Ⓜ️Arbatskaya)

Explore

Meshchansky & Basmanny

Covering a large swathe of Moscow, Meshchansky is a markedly laid-back district, dominated by pre-revolutionary residential buildings. Beyond the Garden Ring, the 19th-century red-brick factories have been taken over by postmodern galleries, cool cafes and digital start-ups. South of the Yauza, Taganskaya pl is a monster intersection that can be difficult to navigate, but the area is home to a few unusual sights.

The Sights in a Day

Begin at Lubyanskaya pl, where the former **KGB building** (p78) looks over a modest stone that marks the millions of people who perished in the infamous Gulag camps. Next, make your way to **Chistye Prudy** (p78) to enjoy a leisurely stroll around the pond. Nearby ul Pokrovka is now one of the city's best restaurant rows, making it a great place for lunch and people-watching.

Head to the other side of the railroad tracks to discover one of Moscow's hottest art, shopping and start-up scenes. The flagship **Winzavod** (p74), a former winery, is packed with galleries, while the nearby **ArtPlay** (p75) area specialises in modern design.

Choose one of the trendy restaurants on ul Maroseyka for dinner, then sample Moscow's contemporary culture at the **Gogol Centre** (p81) or **New Ballet** (p81).

Top Sights

Winzavod & ArtPlay (p74)

Best of Meshchansky & Basmanny

Eating
Kitayskaya Gramota (p80)

Levon's Highland Cuisine (p79)

Darbazi (p79)

Shopping
Izmaylovsky Market (p82)

Khokhlovka Original (p83)

Contemporary Art
Winzavod Centre for Contemporary Art (p74)

Soviet History
Bunker-42 Cold War Museum (p78)

Lubyanka (p78)

Getting There

M Metro Both the purple and orange line have stops at Kitay-Gorod. Three different lines have stops along the Boulevard Ring, most importantly the red line at Chistye Prudy.

M Metro The converted factories are best accessed from Kurskaya at the intersection of the dark-blue, light-green and ring lines.

Top Sights
Winzavod & ArtPlay

A hundred years ago, industrialisation was a buzz word in Moscow, which is why the city is filled with rather imposing centenarian red-brick factories, all of them defunct. Today's buzzword is gentrification, which brings them back into the spotlight. The huge industrial area behind Kursky train station is being redeveloped as a hot spot for modern culture and start-ups.

Винзавод

Map p76, E5

www.winzavod.ru

4-y Syromyatnichesky per 1

admission free

M Chkalovskaya

Exhibition space, Winzavod

Winzavod

It all began with Winzavod, a former wine-bottling factory that was converted into exhibit and studio space for Moscow artists in 2007. Its buildings still bear names such as Fermentation Workshop, but now they are packed with art galleries, funky shops and fashion showrooms. Sadly, politics has forced its flagship, M&J Guelman Gallery, to leave the area, but there are still a few good ones to inspect, particularly the temporary exhibitions housed at Red & White Wine Workshops.

Even if you're not in the market for the art world's next big thing, you can hang out at the cafe or catch a film or a lecture at one of the entertainment venues. The main courtyard is a great place to relax over a drink.

ArtPlay

The nearby Manometer factory has also been touched by the magic wand of gentrification. It is now known as **ArtPlay** (📞495-620 0882; www.artplay.ru; ul Nizhny Syromyatnichesky per 10; admission free; 🕒noon-8pm Tue-Sun). The design centre is home to firms specialising in urban planning and architectural design, as well as furniture showrooms and antique stores. Considering the architectural emphasis, there is perhaps less for the casual caller to see, although there are always diverse and dynamic rotating exhibits in the display spaces. ArtPlay is a bit of a maze, which is now expanding into adjacent industrial spaces.

☑ **Top Tips**

▶ At Artplay, take an elevator to the top of the high-rise building at the very back of the redeveloped space for great views of this scruffy part of the city.

▶ Arma, once a factory producing gas for street lamps, is the newest and largest addition to the scene. Its massive cylindrical towers now mostly contain offices, but there are quite a few nice cafes and a couple of shops in the rapidly developing area.

✕ **Take a Break**

Tsurtsum Cafe (Цурцум кафе; 4-y Syromyatnichesky per 1 str 6; 🕒10am-11pm) is a local institution and a favourite meeting point.

You can also refuel at **Edward's** (ArtPlay, ul Nizhnyaya Syromyatnicheskaya per 10, str 9; 🕒8am-midnight; ⓜChkalovskaya) the smallish pub in the middle of Artplay's maze.

Winzavod Center for Contemporary Art

ul Syromyatnicheskaya
ArtPlay 17

Verkhnyaya Syromyatnicheskaya ul

Chkalovskaya Ⓜ

Nizhnaya Syromyatnicheskaya ul

Yauza River

Nikoloyamskaya nab

Kostomarovsky most

ul Nikoloyamskaya

Pestrovsky per

Bolshoy Drovyanoy per

ul Zemlyanoy val

TAGANKA

Taganskaya Ⓜ

Marksistskaya Ⓜ

Taganskaya Ⓜ

Taganskaya pl

Taganskaya Ⓜ

per Obukha

per Vorontsovo pole

ul Vorontsovo pole

Serebryanicheskaya nab

Bernikovskaya nab

ul Nikoloyamskaya

Ulyanovsky per

5 ✕

Teterinsky per

5-Y Kotelnichesky per

Bunker-42 Cold War Museum 2

rovsky bul

Yauzsky bul

Podkolokolny per

Serebryanichesky per

Ustinsky per

Yauzskaya ul

ul Goncharnaya

Kotelnicheskaya nab

Moscow River

Kosmodamianskaya nab

Khokholovsky per

19

ul Solyanka

Ustinsky per

Moskvoretskaya nab

Sadovnicheskaya ul

Sadovnicheskaya nab

Sadovnicheskaya nab

Ozerkovskaya nab

per

ul Maroseyka

Kitay-Gorod Ⓜ

Kitay-Gorod Ⓜ

Kitaygorodsky proezd

Rauzhskaya nab

Komissariatsky most

Ovchinnikovskaya nab

Runovsky per

Ozerkovsky per

Novokuznetskaya Ⓜ

Gorod

Staraya pl

KITAY-GOROD

Park Zaryadye

For reviews see
◉	Top Sights	p74
⦿	Sights	p78
✕	Eating	p78
🍷	Drinking	p80
✦	Entertainment	p81
🛍	Shopping	p82

Ⓝ

0 — 500 m
0 — 0.25 miles

5

6

7

8

A B C D E

Sights

Lubyanka

HISTORIC BUILDING

1 Map p76, A4

Easily the most feared edifice in Russia, looming on the northeastern side of Lubyanskaya pl is the brain centre behind Stalin's genocidal purges and the network of concentration camps known as Gulag. The building came into life circa 1900 as the headquarters of an insurance company, but was taken over by the CheKa (Bolshevik secret police) in 1919 and remained in the hands of its successors – OGPU, NKVD, MGB and finally KGB. The building is not open to the public. (Лубянка; Lubyanskaya pl; Ⓜ Lubyanka)

Local Life
Chistye Prudy

Othererwise known as the **'Clean Ponds'** (Map 76, C4; Чистые пруды; Chistoprudny bul; Ⓜ Chistye Prudy), Christye Purdy is a lovely little pond that graces the Boulevard Ring at the ul Pokrovka intersection. The Boulevard Ring is always a prime location for strolling, but the quaint pond makes this a particularly desirable address. Paddleboats in summer and ice skating in winter are essential parts of the ambience. Buy a coffee, find a bench or sit on the grass, and watch the world go by.

Bunker-42 Cold War Museum

MUSEUM

2 Map p76, C8

On a quiet side street near Tagan-skaya pl, a nondescript neoclassical building is the gateway to the secret Cold War–era communications centre. The facility was meant to serve as the communications headquarters in the event of a nuclear attack. As such, the building was just a shell, serving as an entryway to the 7000-sq-metre space 60m underground. Now in private hands, the facility has been converted into a sort of a museum dedicated to the Cold War. (☏ 495-500 0554; www.bunker42.com; 5-y Kotelnichesky per 11; tours adult/student from ₽2200/1300; ◷ by appointment; Ⓜ Taganskaya)

Eating

Dukhan Chito-Ra

GEORGIAN $

3 Map p76, E3

It's a blessing when one of the most revered Georgian eateries in town is also one of the cheapest. The object of worship here is *khinkali* – large, meat-filled dumplings – but the traditional vegie starters are also great. The rather inevitable downside is that the place is constantly busy and there is often a queue to get in. (☏ 8-916-393 0030; www.chito-ra.ru; ul Kazakhova 10 str 2; mains ₽300-500; ◷ noon-11pm; Ⓜ Kurskaya)

Bunker-42 Cold War Museum

Levon's Highland Cuisine

ARMENIAN $

4 🍴 Map p76, B4

You might be distracted by the crazy wall paintings, which depict Darth Vader and Chewbacca mingling with characters from the Soviet comedy *Prisoner of the Caucasus*, but the main part in this film-themed mayhem is reserved for *brtuch* – a wrap made of Armenian flat bread and chicken with a choice of gravy – pomegranate, walnut or garlicky yogurt. (☎8-985-108 8947; http://levonscafe.com/; ul Pokrovka 3/7 str 1a; wraps ₽250; ☺10am-11pm; Ⓜ Kitay-Gorod)

Darbazi

GEORGIAN $$

5 🍴 Map p76, C7

The vast majority of Georgian restaurants focus on the most popular, tried-and-true fare, such as shashlyk (meat kebabs) and *khinkali* (dumplings). This classy place goes far beyond these, listing less well-known delicacies with almost encyclopedic meticulousness. Our favourite is *chakapuli* (lamb cooked in white wine with tarragon) and *megreli kharcho* (duck in walnut sauce). (☎495-915 3632; www.darbazirest.ru; ul Nikoloyamskaya 16; mains ₽590-1500; ☺noon-midnight; 🛜; Ⓜ Taganskaya)

Local Life

Liudi Kak Liudi

An old institution, **Liudi Kak Liudi**
(Map p76, A5) Люди как люди; www.
ludikakludi.ru; Solyansky tupik 1/4; mains
₽150-300; 9am-11pm Sun-Wed, 9am
to dawn Thu-Sat; Kitay-Gorod) is a
quaint cafe that has for decades
served as a pit stop for Kitay Gorod
club-goers. During the day, it's a
pleasant place to get a quick bite
and a coffee or smoothie.

Kitayskaya Gramota   CHINESE $$

6   Map p76, A3

Ignore the fact that the waitstaff are
dressed as Mao's soldiers; this is the
place to try outstanding Cantonese
fare in an atmosphere echoing that
of the opium war's decadence. A true
culinary magician, the Chinese chef
turns any ingredient – from hog paw
to octopus to simple milk – into a
mouth-watering delicacy. (Китайская
грамота; 495-625 4757; http://chinagra
mota.ru/; ul Sretenka 1; mains ₽400-1200;
noon-midnight; Sretenskaya)

Odessa-Mama   UKRAINIAN $$

7   Map p76, B4

Come here to celebrate Odessa,
affectionately called 'Mama' by the
residents of this port city. What Mama
cooks is a wild fusion of Jewish,
Ukrainian and Balkan foods, with a
strong emphasis on Black Sea fish. It's
like island hopping – from *forshmak*
(Jewish herring pate) to Ukrainian

borsch and eventually to fried Odessa
gobies. (8-964-647 1110; www.cafeodessa.
ru; per Krivokolenny 10 str 5; ₽400-800;
10am-11pm Sun-Thu, to 2am Fri & Sat;
Chistye Prudy)

Drinking

Sisters Cafe   CAFE

8   Map p76, B4

This cosy and quiet cafe-bar has a
distinct feminine touch about it – as
if Chekhov's sisters have finally made
their way to Moscow and started a
new life here. Cheapish smoothies,
lemonades and teas are on offer, but
the wine and cocktail lists are equally
impressive. (495-623 0932; www.cafe
sisters.com; ul Pokrovka 6; noon-11pm;
Kitay-Gorod)

Ukuleleshnaya   BAR

9   Map p76, C4

In its new location, this is now more
of a bar than a musical instrument
shop, although ukuleles still adorn
the walls, prompting an occasional
jam session. Craft beer prevails on
the drinks list, but Ukuleleshnaya
also serves experimental cocktails
of its own invention. Live concerts
happen regularly and resident
Pomeranian Spitz Berseny (cute dog)
presides over the resulting madness.
(Укулелешная; 495-642 5726; www.
uku-uku.ru; ul Pokrovka 17 str 1; noon-
midnight Sun-Thu, noon-4am Fri & Sat;
Chistye Prudy)

Coffee Bean
CAFE

10 Map p76, C4

Winds of change brought US national Jerry Ruditser to Moscow in the early 1990s on a mission to create the nation's first coffee chain, which he succeeded in doing long before Starbucks found Russia on the map. Some argue it's still the best coffee served in the capital. That might be disputed, but on the friendliness front Coffee Bean is unbeatable. (www.coffeebean.ru; ul Pokrovka 21; ◷8am-11pm; Ⓜ Chistye Prudy)

Chaynaya Vysota
TEAHOUSE

11 Map p76, C4

Tearoom? Gelateria? This place looks more like an academic library of tea and ice cream, an impression enhanced by it sharing premises with a bookshop. The tea menu is an endless list of pu'ers and oolongs, while ice-cream flavours represent everything that grows in the former USSR – from gooseberry or fir-needle juice to chestnuts and Crimean rose petals. (Чайная высота; http://cha108.ru/; ul Pokrovka 27 str 1; 🛜; Ⓜ Chistye Prudy)

Cafe Didu
BAR

12 Map p76, B3

This playful club-cafe invites relaxation and fun with lounge furniture, tantalising cocktails and colourful modelling clay. Containers of pliable playdough are found on each table (right next to the condiments) and the sculpted results are on display all around the restaurant. (☎495-624 1320; www.cafe-didu.ru; Myasnitskaya ul 24; ◷noon-6am; 🛜 ♿; Ⓜ Chistye Prudy)

Entertainment

Gogol Centre
THEATRE

13 ⭐ Map p76, E4

One of the most talked about theatres in Moscow is under constant political pressure due to the non-conformist position of its director Kirill Serebrennikov. Gogol Centre is a modern venue that hosts many musical and dance performances as well as cutting-edge drama. The latter is difficult to appreciate without knowing Russian. (Гоголь-центр; ☎499-262 9214; www.gogolcenter.com; ul Kazakhova 8; Ⓜ Kurskaya)

New Ballet
DANCE

14 ⭐ Map p76, E2

If you can't stand to see another *Swan Lake,* you will be pleased to know that the New Ballet performs innovative contemporary dance. This performance art, called 'plastic ballet', incorporates elements of classical and modern dance, as well as pantomime and drama. The theatre is tiny, providing a close-up look at original, cutting-edge choreography. (☎495-265 7510; www.newballet.ru; Novaya Basmannaya ul 25/2; ◷box office 11am-7pm; Ⓜ Krasnye Vorota)

Pirogi on Maroseyka

LIVE MUSIC, CINEMA

15 ⭐ Map p76, A4

If you have ever visited Pirogi's earlier incarnations, you might be surprised by the club's slick storefront. Inside, it's not dark and it's not grungy. Do not fear, however, as the crucial elements have not changed: decent food, affordable beer and movies and music every night, all of which draw the young, broke and beautiful. (https://pirogicafe.ru; ul Maroseyka 9/2; ⊗24hr; 🛜; Ⓜ Kitay-Gorod)

Gazgolder

LIVE MUSIC

16 ⭐ Map p76, E4

A popular concert venue, associated with a namesake label that's responsible for one of Russia's best-known rap acts, Basta. (📞495-741 8383; http://gazgolder.com; Nizhny Susalny per 5 str 26; Ⓜ Kurskaya)

Shopping

Naivno? Ochen!

HOMEWARES

17 🔒 Map p76, E6

These folks do a great service selling souvenirs – cups, plates and T-shirts – themed on inspired and whismical drawings produced by children with special needs. Proceeds go to charities that help them. It's a big deal for a country that lags far behind the West on that front. (Наивно? Очень!; 📞499-678 0162; www.orz-design.ru; ArtPlay, ul Nizhnyaya Syromyatnicheskaya per 10; ⊗11am-10pm; Ⓜ Kurksaya)

Understand

Izmaylovsky Market

Surrounding the faux 'tsar's palace' (pictured on p72), **Izmaylovsky Market** (www.kremlin-izmailovo.com; Izmaylovskoye sh 73; ⊗10am-8pm; Ⓜ Partizanskaya) is the ultimate place to shop for *matryoshka* dolls, military uniforms, icons, Soviet badges, and some real antiques. Huge and diverse, it is almost a theme park, including shops, cafes and a couple of not terribly exciting museums.

Serious antiquarians occupy the 2nd floor of the wooden trade row surrounding the palace, but for really good stuff you need to come here at an ungodly hour on Saturday morning and compete with pros from Moscow galleries. Keep in mind that Russia bans the export of any item older than 100 years. Feel free to negotiate, but don't expect vendors to come down more than 10%.

The famous flea market is only part of a big **theme park** (Кремль в Измайлово), which includes shops, restaurants, museums and monuments, all contained within a mock 'kremlin' (complete with walls and towers that make a great photo op). Within the kremlin walls, the place recreates the workshops and trade rows of an old settlement.

Souvenirs for sale at Izmaylovsky Market

Odensya Dlya Schastya

CLOTHING

18 🔒 Map p76, C4

This sweet boutique – encouraging shoppers to 'dress for happiness' – carries unique clothing by a few distinctive designers, including Moscow native Oleg Biryukov. The designer's eponymous label features refined styles with long, flowing lines and subdued, solid colours. The tastefulness and elegance exemplify the new direction of Russian fashion. (Оденься для счастья; ul Pokrovka 31; ⊙11am-9pm; Ⓜ Kurskaya)

Khokhlovka Original

CLOTHING

19 🔒 Map p76, B5

This is about the most clandestine fashion store we've ever reviewed. To get in, enter a graffiti-covered courtyard, then look for a small gap between two single-storey buildings on your left – the door is inside the tiny passage. The small showroom displays clothes and accessories produced by dozens of young (but often stellar) Russian designers. (http:// hhlvk.ru; Khokhlovsky per 7; ⊙noon-10pm; Ⓜ Kitay-Gorod)

Top Sights
Park Pobedy

Getting There

Ⓜ From the centre, take line 3 (dark blue) to Park Pobedy. Or from the International Business Centre (Delovoy Tsentr), take the new yellow line 8A to Park Pobedy.

Magnificent Park Pobedy (Victory Park) at Poklonnaya Hill is a huge memorial complex commemorating the sacrifice and celebrating the triumph of the Great Patriotic War – as WWII is known in Russia. Unveiled on the 50th anniversary of the victory, the park includes endless fountains, monuments and museums, as well as a memorial church, synagogue and mosque.

Obelisk

The park's dominant monument is an enormous obelisk, topped with a sculpture of St George slaying the dragon (the work of contemporary Moscow artist Zurab Tsereteli). Its height is exactly 141.8m, with every 10cm representing one day of the war. For the 60th anniversary of Victory Day in 2005, President Vladimir Putin unveiled 15 mighty bronze cannons, symbolic of the war's 15 fronts.

Museum of the Great Patriotic War

The **Museum of the Great Patriotic War** (Центральный музей Великой Отечественной Войны; victorymuseum.ru; ul Bratiev Fonchenko 10; adult/child ₽300/200; ⊘10am-6pm Tue-Sun Nov-Mar, to 8pm Apr-Oct) is the centrepiece of Park Pobedy.

The massive museum has hundreds of exhibits, including dioramas of every major WWII battle the Russians fought in, as well as weapons, photographs, documents and other wartime memorabilia.

The museum building also contains two impressive memorial rooms: the Hall of Glory honours the many heroes of the Soviet Union, while the moving Hall of Remembrance & Sorrow is hung with strings of glass-bead 'teardrops' in memory of the fallen.

Exposition of Military Equipment

Tucked into a corner of the vast Park Pobedy, the **Exposition of Military Equipment** (Площадка боевой техники; victorymuseum.ru; adult/child ₽300/200; ⊘11am-6pm Tue-Sun) displays weapons and military equipment from the WWII era. There are plenty of Red Army tanks, armoured cars and self-propelled artillery, not to mention the famous Katyusha rocket launcher. You'll also see train cars used by the civil engineering unit, fighter planes and navel destroyers.

Парк Победы

www.poklonnaya-gora.ru

Kutuzovsky pr

admission free

⊘ dawn-dusk

🚻

Ⓜ Park Pobedy

☑ Top Tips

▶ Park Pobedy covers a vast area, so a thorough tour of its monuments, museums and other features entails a lot of walking. Bicycles are available to rent (from ₽250 per hour).

▶ The many attractions for children include a great playground and a small amusement park.

✗ Take a Break

Grab a quick bite at one of the many fast-food kiosks selling hot dogs, pizza and the like.

There are no standout restaurants in the vicinity, but you can get a satisfactory sit-down meal at one of the nearby chain cafes.

Explore
St Petersburg

Historic Heart.............................. 88

Sennaya, Kolomna
& Vasilyevsky Island.................. 106

Smolny & Vosstaniya................. 122

Petrograd & Vyborg Sides.......... 134

Worth a Trip
The Soviet South.................................... 146

Jordan Staircase at the Winter Palace (p91), State Hermitage
Museum
MARCO RUBINO/SHUTTERSTOCK ©

Explore

Historic Heart

Radiating out from the golden spire of the Admiralty towards the Fontanka River, the Historic Heart has plenty of obvious attractions, such as the Hermitage, Russian Museum and the Church on the Spilled Blood, not to mention the city's most famous avenue: Nevsky Prospekt. There are also quirky gems and lovely parks.

The Sights in a Day

☀ For an unforgettable first impression, head straight to vast Palace Sq: on one side is the **Winter Palace** (p91), home to the main collection of the Hermitage; on the other is the sweeping grandeur of the **General Staff Building** (p94), its east wing housing the Hermitage's amazing stash of Impressionist and post-Impressionist works. Take your pick from these two collections and spend the morning in awestruck, art-immersed wonder.

☀ From here, cherry-pick your way through the rest of the neighbourhood. The dazzling but incongruous **Church of the Saviour on the Spilled Blood** (p96) is an obligatory stop, as is the splendid view from the cupola of **St Isaac's Cathedral** (p100). When you need a breather, take a break from the hubbub in the lush Summer Garden or Mikhailovsky Garden.

☾ In the evening, find high-class entertainment in the theatres around pl Iskusstv and pl Ostrovskogo or head to the clubs and cocktails bars that are often hidden away in unexpected places.

 Top Sights

State Hermitage Museum (p90)

Church of the Saviour on the Spilled Blood (p96)

♥ Best of the Historic Heart

Eating
Gräs x Madbaren (p102)

Cococo (p103)

Yat (p102)

Gogol (p102)

Drinking
Top Hops (p103)

Borodabar (p103)

Coffee 22 (p103)

Getting There

Ⓜ **Metro** The neighbourhood's three metro stations include the interconnecting Nevsky Prospekt (line 2) and Gostiny Dvor (line 3), and Admiralteyskaya (line 5) near the Hermitage.

🚎 **Trolleybus** Bus 7 runs the length of Nevsky pr, past Palace Sq and across to Vasilyevsky Island.

🚌 **Bus** Hop on bus 7, 10, 24, 27, 181 or 191 to save some footwork along Nevsky.

Top Sights
State Hermitage Museum

The geographic and tourism centrepiece of St Petersburg is one of the world's greatest art collections and usually most visitors' first stop in the city, even if it is simply to admire the baroque Winter Palace and the extraordinary ensemble of buildings that surround it. No other institution so embodies the opulence and extravagance of the Romanovs.

Государственный Эрмитаж

⊙ Map p98, B2

www.hermitagemuseum.org

Dvortsovaya pl 2

combined ticket ₽700

🕐 10.30am-6pm Tue, Thu, Sat & Sun, to 9pm Wed & Fri

Ⓜ Admiralteyskaya

Winter Palace

The Collection

The Hermitage first opened to the public in 1852. Today, for the price of admission, anybody can parade down the grand staircases and across parquet floors, gawping at crystal chandeliers, gilded furniture and an amazing art collection that once was for the tsar's court's eyes only.

The Western European Collection, in particular, does not miss much: Spanish, Flemish, Dutch, French, English and German art are all covered from the 15th to the 18th centuries, while the Italian collection goes back all the way to the 13th century, including the Florentine and Venetian Renaissance, with priceless works by Leonardo da Vinci, Raphael, Michelangelo and Titian. A highlight is the enormous collection of Dutch and Flemish paintings, in particular the spectacular assortment of Rembrandt, most notably his masterpiece *Return of the Prodigal Son*.

Winter Palace

The **Winter Palace** (Зимний дворец) is a stunning mint-green, white and gold profusion of columns, windows and recesses, with its roof topped by rows of classical statues. It was commissioned from in 1754 by Empress Elizabeth. Catherine the Great and her successors had most of the interior remodelled in a classical style by 1837. It remained an imperial home until 1917, though the last two tsars spent more time in other palaces.

Today you can tour the palace's grand reception halls and chambers, and wander gallery after gallery stuffed with Eurasian and Asian antiquities, as well as collections of European and Eastern paintings, sculptures and decorative arts.

For lovers of things that glitter and the applied arts, the Hermitage's **Treasure Gallery** (☎812-571 8446; Winter Palace, tour of Diamond or Golden Rooms ₽350) should not be missed. Its two special collections, guarded behind vault doors, are open only

☑ **Top Tips**

▶ Avoid long entrance queues by buying your ticket online. The printed-out voucher or PDF on a wi-fi-enabled device is valid for 180 days.

▶ With an early start you can see some of the main Hermitage and the General Staff Building in a day – if that's your plan buy the combined day ticket that gives access to both museums.

▶ Backpacks are not allowed in the Hermitage.

✗ **Take a Break**

Eating options in the Hermitage are limited to busy self-serve cafes on the ground-floor corridor, between the foot of the Jordan staircase and Room 100.

The General Staff Building's **Cafe Hermitage** (Кафе Эрмитаж; ☎812-703 7528; General Staff Builidng, 8 Dvortsovaya pl; mains ₽250-450; ⏱11am-11pm Tue, Thu, Sat & Sun, until 8pm Wed & Fri) is a pleasant self-serve place.

One of the Treasure Gallery's Golden Rooms (p91)

by guided tour, for which you should either call ahead to reserve a place, or buy a ticket at the entrance.

Small & Large Hermitage

The classical Small Hermitage, which evolved from a series of buildings constructed between Palace Sq and the Neva between 1764 and 1769, was used by Catherine the Great as a retreat and to house the art collection started by Peter the Great, which she significantly expanded. On the building's 1st floor, connecting the two sides, is the Hanging Garden overlooked by ceremonial Pavilion Hall hung with 28 chandeliers. Here you'll find the incredible Peacock Clock and a wonderful copy of a Roman floor mosaic.

Facing the Neva, the Great (Old) Hermitage (also known as the Large Hermitage) dates from the time of Catherine the Great. It mainly houses Italian Rennaissance art including works by Leonardo da Vinci, Raphael, Titian, Giorgione, Botticelli, Caravaggio and Tiepolo.

New Hermitage

Facing Millionnaya ul, the New Hermitage was built for Nicholas II in 1852, to hold the growing art collection and as a museum for the public. Designed by German neoclassicist

The Hermitage – Ground Floor

New Hermitage

Atlantes

State Staircase

Greek & Roman Antiquities (Rooms 106–131)

Treasury Gallery: Diamond Rooms (Room 126)

Council Staircase

Small Hermitage

Millionnaya ul

Dvortsovaya nab

Ancient Egypt (Room 100)

Lift

Jordan Staircase

Cafe

Cafe

Hermitage Shop

Rastrelli Gallery

Cafe

Audioguide

Excursions Office

Ticket Control

Ticket Machines

Group Entrance

Ticket Booths

Winter Palace Courtyard

Main Entrance

Dvortsovaya pl

Friends of the Hermitage; Information Desk

Ticket Machines

Cloakroom Area

Prehistoric Artefacts (Rooms 11–24, 27 & 33)

Siberian Antiquities (Rooms 26–32)

Central Asia & Caucasus (Rooms 38–69)

Treasure Gallery: Golden Rooms (41–45)

Flemish Art section (p91)

architect and painter Von Klenze, the historically preserved rooms house collections of ancient art, European paintings, sculptures and decorative art.

On the building's 1st floor is Room 227, a gallery designed by Giacomo Quarenghi in 1792 to house the *Raphael Loggias*, copies of the original frescoes in the Vatican, Rome, that had so impressed Catherine the Great on her visit there.

General Staff Building

The east wing of this magnificent **building** (Здание Главного штаба; Dvortsovaya pl 6-8; ₽300, incl main Hermitage museum & other buildings ₽700), wrapping around

the south of Palace Sq and designed by Carlo Rossi in the 1820s, marries immaculately restored interiors with contemporary architecture to create a series of galleries displaying the Hermitage's amazing collection of Impressionist and post-Impressionist works. Contemporary works are displayed here, too, often in temporary exhibitions by major artists.

Entry to the galleries is via a broad new marble staircase, which doubles as an amphitheatre for musical performances held in the glassed-over courtyard.

The Hermitage – 1st Floor

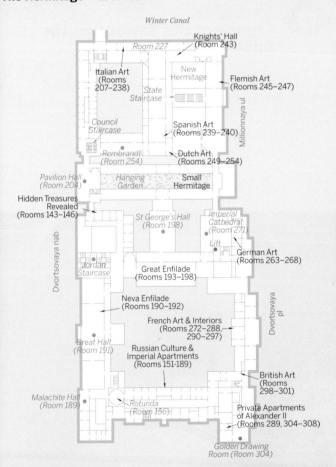

Winter Canal

Room 227

Knights' Hall
(Room 243)

Italian Art
(Rooms
207–238)

New
Hermitage

Flemish Art
(Rooms 245–247)

State
Staircase

Council
Staircase

Spanish Art
(Rooms 239–240)

Rembrandt
(Room 254)

Dutch Art
(Rooms 249–254)

Millionnaya ul

Pavilion Hall
(Room 204)

Hanging
Garden

Small
Hermitage

Hidden Treasures
Revealed
(Rooms 143–146)

St George's Hall
(Room 198)

Imperial
Cathedral
(Room 271)

Dvortsovaya nab

Lift

German Art
(Rooms 263–268)

Jordan
Staircase

Great Enfilade
(Rooms 193–198)

Neva Enfilade
(Rooms 190–192)

French Art & Interiors
(Rooms 272–288,
290–297)

Dvortsovaya pl

Great Hall
(Room 191)

Russian Culture &
Imperial Apartments
(Rooms 151–189)

Malachite Hall
(Room 189)

Rotunda
(Room 156)

British Art
(Rooms
298–301)

Private Apartments
of Alexander II
(Rooms 289, 304–308)

Golden Drawing
Room (Room 304)

Top Sights
Church of the Saviour on the Spilled Blood

This five-domed dazzler is St Petersburg's most elaborate church, with a classic Russian Orthodox exterior and an interior decorated with some 7000 sq metres of mosaics.

Церковь Спаса на Крови

Map p98, E2

http://eng.cathedral.ru/spasa_na_krovi/

Konyushennaya pl

adult/student ₽250/150

10.30am–6pm Thu-Tue

M Nevsky Prospekt

Ceiling mosaics

History

Officially called the Church of the Resurrection of Christ, its colloquial name references the assassination attempt on Tsar Alexander II here in 1881. The church, which was was consecrated in 1907, incorporates elements of 18th-century Russian architecture from Moscow and Yaroslavl, and is so lavish it took 24 years to build and went over budget by one million roubles – an enormous sum for the times.

Interior

Decades of abuse and neglect during most of the Soviet era ended in the 1970s when restoration began. When the doors reopened 27 years later on what is now a museum, visitors were astounded by the spectacular mosaics covering the walls and ceilings. Designs for the mosaics came from top artists of the day including Victor Vasnetsov, Mikhail Nesterov and Andrey Ryabushkin.

Exterior

The polychromatic exterior – decorated with mosaics of detailed scenes from the New Testament and the coats of arms of the provinces, regions and towns of the Russian Empire of Alexander's time – is equally showstopping. Twenty granite plaques around the facade record the main events of Alexander's reign.

☑ Top Tips

▶ In the western apse, the spot of the assassination attempt on Tsar Alexander II is marked by a small but beautiful canopy made of rhodonite and jasper.

▶ Near the exit is a small exhibition of photos showing parts of the restoration process.

✕ Take a Break

Fuel up cheaply at Marketplace (p102), a contemporary-styled self-serve cafeteria.

Enjoy a vegetarian meal at **Ukrop** (☎812-946 3035; www.cafe-ukrop. ru; Malaya Konyushennaya ul 14; mains ₽280-360; ☺9am-11pm; 🛜🖉; Ⓜ Nevsky Prospekt).

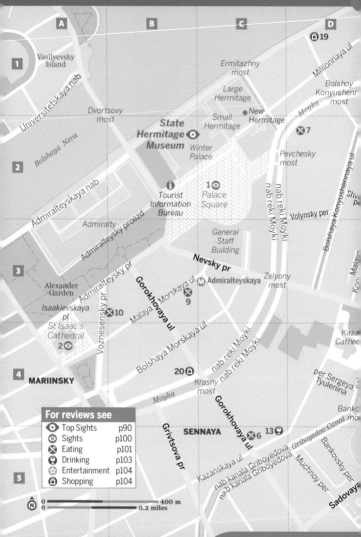

For reviews see

⊙	Top Sights	p90
⊙	Sights	p100
⊗	Eating	p101
⊗	Drinking	p103
⊛	Entertainment	p104
⊕	Shopping	p104

E

F

nab Lebyazhey kanavki

⊙5
Summer
Garden

Mars
Field

nab reki Fontanki

G

SMOLNY

H

Mokhovaya ul

ul Pestelya

1

eatralny
most

nab reki Moyki

1-y
Sadovy
most

1-y
Inzhenerny
most

Panteleymonovsky
most

LITEYNY

nab reki Fontanki

Mokhovaya ul

Liteyny pr

2

shennaya
l

**⊙ Church of the Saviour
on the Spilled Blood**

3⊙ Russian
Museum

Mikhailovsky
Gardens

Mikhailovsky
Castle

Zamkovaya

St Petersburg
State Circus

most
Belinskogo ul Belinskogo

riboyedova

16☆

Pl Iskusstv

Italiyanskaya ul

⊙8

Inzhenernaya ul

nab reki Fontanki

ul Karavannaya

3

Nevsky
Prospekt

Nevsky pr

Mikhaylovskaya ul

Sadovaya ul

Tourist
Information
Bureau **ⓘ**

Manezhnaya
pl

⊙15

⊙18

Malaya Sadovay ul

Fabergé
Museum **4
⊙**

**Gostiny
Dvor**

Ⓜ

Gostiny
Dvor

Ⓜ

National
Library
of Russia

pl Ostrovskogo

Anichkov
Palace

Anichkov
most

Nevsky pr

4

msova

Sadovaya ul

per Krylova

17☆

Vorontsov
Palace

ul Zodchego Rossi

ul Lomonosova

**12
⊙**

nab reki Fontanki

Grafsky per

nab reki Fontanki

VOSSTANIYA

Vladimirsky pr

5

Sights

Palace Square SQUARE

1 Map p98, C2

This vast expanse is simply one of the most striking squares in the world, still redolent of imperial grandeur almost a century after the end of the Romanov dynasty. For the most amazing first impression, walk from Nevsky pr, up Bolshaya Morskaya ul and under the **triumphal arch**. (Дворцовая площадь; Dvortsovaya pl; Ⓜ Admiralteyskaya)

St Isaac's Cathedral MUSEUM

2 Map p98, A4

The golden dome of St Isaac's Cathedral dominates the St Petersburg skyline. Its obscenely lavish interior is open as a museum, although services are held in the cathedral throughout the year. Most people bypass the

✅ Top Tip
Raising of the Bridges

It's quite a sight to witness the raising of the bridges over the Neva river during the navigation period. **Dvortsovy most** (Map p98, A1; Palace Bridge; Дворцовый мост; Ⓜ Admiralteyskaya), beside the Winter Palace, is one of the most popular spots to watch this event as there is classical music broadcast and a carnival atmosphere with street vendors and plenty of sightseeing boats bobbing in the Neva.

museum to climb the 262 steps to the *kolonnada* (colonnade) around the drum of the dome, providing superb city views. (Исаакиевский собор; ☑ 812-315 9732; www.cathedral.ru; Isaakievskaya pl; cathedral adult/student ₽250/150, colonnade ₽150; ⏱ cathedral 10.30am-10.30pm Thu-Tue May-Sep, to 6pm Oct-Apr, colonnade 10.30am-10.30pm May-Oct, to 6pm Nov-Apr; Ⓜ Admiralteyskaya)

Russian Museum MUSEUM

3 Map p98, F2

Focusing solely on Russian art, from ancient church icons to 20th-century paintings, the Russian Museum's collection is magnificent and can easily be viewed in half a day or less. The collection includes works by Karl Bryullov, Alexander Ivanov, Nicholas Ghe, Ilya Repin, Natalya Goncharova, Kazimir Malevich and Kuzma Petrov-Vodkin, among many others, and the masterpieces keep on coming as you tour the beautiful Carlo Rossi–designed Mikhailovsky Palace and its attached wings. (Русский музей; ☑ 812-595 4248; www.rusmuseum.ru; Inzhenernaya ul 4; adult/student ₽450/200; ⏱ 10am-8pm Mon, 10am-6pm Wed & Fri-Sun, 1-9pm Thu; Ⓜ Nevsky Prospekt)

Fabergé Museum MUSEUM

4 Map p98, G4

The magnificently restored Shuvalovsky Palace is home to the world's largest collection of pieces (including nine imperial Easter eggs) manufactured by the jeweller Peter Carl

Renaissance Imperial Egg, Fabergé Museum

Fabergé and fellow master craftsmen and -women of pre-revolutionary Russia. (Музей Фаберже; ☏812-333 2655; http://fabergemuseum.ru; nab reki Fontanki 21; ₽450, incl tour ₽600; ☺10am-8.45pm Sat-Thur; Ⓜ Gostiny Dvor)

Summer Garden
PARK

 5 Map p98, F1

The city's oldest park, these leafy, shady gardens can be entered either at the northern Neva or southern Moyka end. Early-18th-century architects designed the garden in a Dutch baroque style, following a geometric plan, with fountains, pavilions and sculptures studding the grounds. The ornate cast-iron fence along the Neva side was a later addition, built between 1771

and 1784. (Летний сад; ☏812-314 0374; https://igardens.ru; nab reki Moyki; tours from ₽1200; ☺10am-10pm May-Sep, 10am-8pm Oct-Mar, closed Apr; Ⓜ Gostiny Dvor)

Eating

Zoom Café
EUROPEAN $

6 Map p98, C5

A perennially popular cafe (expect to wait for a table at peak times) with a cosy feel and an interesting menu, ranging from Japanese-style chicken in teriyaki sauce to potato pancakes with salmon and cream cheese. Well-stocked bookshelves, a range of board games and adorable cuddly toys (each with its own name) encourage

---

Understand
Stolovaya

Locals still disappear to their local *stolovaya* (столовая; canteen) at lunchtime for a supremely cheap and social meal, albeit one that's rarely particularly exciting. These places, hangovers from the Soviet days, are usually sign-posted in Cyrillic and tend to be located in basements and courtyards, but if you stumble across one (look for the sign 'столовая'), you're normally more than welcome to go in. Experiences don't come much more local than this, and you'll usually find yourself saving plenty of cash if you eat in such places.

A sign of their enduring popularity is the recent reinvention of the *stolovaya* in such guises as **Marketplace** (Map p98, D3; http://market-place.me; Nevsky pr 24; mains ₽200-300; ⊙8am-5.30am; 🖥🖉; Ⓜ Nevsky Prospekt) – modern, attractive spaces that have taken the essential idea of a *stolovaya* and translated it into something appealing for the contemporary Russian diner.

---

lingering. (🛈812-612 1329; www.cafezoom.ru; Gorokhovaya ul 22; mains ₽350-550; ⊙9am-midnight Mon-Fri, from 11am Sat, from 1pm Sun; 🖥🖉🛉; Ⓜ Nevsky Prospekt)

Yat RUSSIAN $$

 7 Map p98, D2

Perfectly placed for eating near the Hermitage, this country-cottage-style restaurant has an appealing menu of traditional dishes, presented with aplomb. The *shchi* (cabbage-based soup) is excellent, and there is also a great range of flavoured vodkas. There's a fab kids' area with pet rabbits for them to feed. (Ять; 🛈812-957 0023; www.eatinyat.com; nab reki Moyki 16; mains ₽370-750; ⊙11am-11pm; 🖥🛉; Ⓜ Admiralteyskaya)

Gräs x Madbaren FUSION $$

8 Map p98, F3

Anton Abrezov is the talented exec chef behind this Scandi-cool meets Russian locavore restaurant where you can sample dishes such as a delicious corned-beef salad with black garlic and pickled vegetables or an upmarket twist on ramen noodles with succulent roast pork. (🛈812-928 1818; http://grasmadbaren.com; ul Inzhenernaya 7; mains ₽420-550, tasting menu ₽2500; ⊙1-11pm Sun-Thu, until 1am Fri & Sat; 🖥; Ⓜ Gostiny Dvor)

Gogol RUSSIAN $$

 9 Map p98, B3

Like its sibling restaurant Chekov, Gogol whisks diners back to the genteel days of pre-revolutionary Russian home dining. The menu comes in a novel, with chapters for each of the traditional courses. Salads, soups, dumplings and classics such as chicken Kiev are all very well done and served in charming, small dining rooms. (Гоголь; 🛈812-312 6097; http://restaurant-gogol.ru; Malaya Morskaya ul 8; mains ₽350-690; ⊙9am-3am; 🖥; Ⓜ Admiralteyskaya)

Cococo
RUSSIAN $$$

10 Map p98, B3

Cococo has charmed locals with its inventive approach to contemporary Russian cuisine. Your food is likely to arrive disguised as, say, a small bird's egg, a can of peas or a broken flower pot – all rather gimmicky, theatrical and fun. The best way to sample what it does is with its tasting menu (₽2900). Bookings are advised. (☎812-418 2060; www.kokoko.spb.ru; Voznesensky pr 6; mains ₽650-1300; ⊙7-11am, 2pm-1am; 🛜; Ⓜ Admiralteyskaya)

Drinking

Apotheke Bar
COCKTAIL BAR

11 Map p98, E5

The antithesis of the nearby dive bars, Apotheke is a calm, cosy cocoon for cocktail connoisseurs. Its slogan is 'think what you drink' so there's no official menu but a friendly young bartender, most likely in a white jacket and sporting a hipster moustache, to make suggestions or simply surprise you. (☎812-337 1535; http://hatgroup.ru/apotheke-bar; ul Lomonosova 1; ⊙8pm-6am Tue-Sun; Ⓜ Gostiny Dvor)

Top Hops
CRAFT BEER

12 Map p98, F5

One of the nicer craft-beer bars in town, this riverside space with friendly staff serves up a regularly changing menu of 20 beers on tap and scores more in bottles. The tasty Mexican snacks and food (go for nachos and chilli) go down exceptionally well while you sample your way through their range. (☎8-966-757 0116; www.tophops.ru; nab reki Fontanki 55; ⊙4pm-1am Mon-Thu, 2pm-2am Fri-Sun; 🛜; Ⓜ Gostiny Dvor)

Borodabar
COCKTAIL BAR

13 Map p98, C5

Boroda means beard in Russian, and sure enough you'll see plenty of facial hair and tattoos in this hipster cocktail hang-out. Never mind, as the mixologists really know their stuff – we can particularly recommend their smoked Old Fashioned, which is infused with tobacco smoke, and their colourful (and potent) range of shots. (☎911 923 8940; www.facebook.com/Borodabar; Kazanskaya ul 11; ⊙5pm-2am Sun-Thu, to 6am Fri & Sat; 🛜; Ⓜ Nevsky Prospekt)

Local Life
Coffee 22

In an area heavily saturated with hipster cafes, **Coffee 22** (Map p98, C5; https://vk.com/coffeeat22; ul Kazanskaya 22; ⊙8.30am-11pm Mon-Thu, until 1am Fri, 10am-1am Sat, 10am-11pm Sun; 🛜; Ⓜ Nevsky Prospekt) – with its tattooed baristas, arty decor (piercing portrait of poet Jospeh Brodsky, a rustic wall of dried mosses) and fashion-forward customers – is perhaps the hippest of them all. Listen to its DJs via its http://mixcloud.com/coffee22 soundtrack.

Mod Club   BAR, CLUB

14 📍 Map p98, E2

A popular spot for students and other
indie types who appreciate the fun
and friendly atmosphere and a cool
mix of music both live and spun.
Laid-back and great fun, this is a solid
choice for a night out. (www.modclub.
info; nab kanala Griboyedova 7; cover ₽150-
350; ⏰6pm-6am; Ⓜ Nevsky Prospekt)

Kabinet   COCKTAIL BAR

15 📍 Map p98, G4

Bookings are essential for this speak-
easy cocktail bar styled as a secret pok-
er joint and hidden beneath the Grill
Brothers burger restaurant. It's a fun,
sophisticated place with the waiters
dealing sets of cards to determine your
choice of cocktail. (☎8-911-921 1944; www.
instagram.com/kabinet_bar; Malaya Sadovaya
ul 8; ⏰8am-6pm; Ⓜ Gostiny Dvor)

🔍 Local Life

Nevsky Prospekt

Nevsky Prospekt is Russia's most
famous street, running 4km from
the Admiralty to Alexander Nevsky
Monastery, from which it takes its
name. The inner 2.5km to Moscow
Station is the city's shopping centre and focus of its entertainment
and street life. Walking Nevsky is
an essential St Petersburg experience. You'll find yourself back on its
broad, busy pavements throughout
your visit, popping in and out of
shops and lingering at cafes.

Entertainment

Mikhailovsky Theatre   PERFORMING ARTS

16 ⭐ Map p98, E3

This illustrious stage delivers the
Russian ballet or operatic experience,
complete with multi-tiered theatre,
frescoed ceiling and elaborate productions. Pl Iskusstv (Arts Sq) is a lovely
setting for this respected venue, which
is home to the State Academic Opera
& Ballet Company. (Михайловский
театр; ☎812-595 4305; www.mikhailovsky.
ru; pl Iskusstv 1; tickets ₽500-5000;
Ⓜ Nevsky Prospekt)

Alexandrinsky Theatre   THEATRE

17 ⭐ Map p98, F5

This magnificent venue is just one
part of an immaculate architectural
ensemble designed by Carlo Rossi.
The theatre's interior oozes 19th-
century elegance and style, and it's
worth taking a peek even if you don't
see a production here. (☎812-710 4103;
www.alexandrinsky.ru; pl Ostrovskogo 2;
tickets ₽900-6000; Ⓜ Gostiny Dvor)

Shopping

Kupetz Eliseevs   FOOD & DRINKS

18 🔒 Map p98, G4

This Style Moderne stunner is St Petersburg's most elegant grocery store
selling plenty of branded goods from
blends of tea to caviar and handmade

Au Pont Rouge

chocolates as well as delicious freshly baked breads, pastries and cakes. Kids will love watching the animatronic figures in the window display and there are pleasant cafes on the ground floor and in the former wine cellar. (📞 812-456 6666; www.kupetzeliseevs.ru; Nevsky pr 56; ⊙10am-11pm; 🛜; Ⓜ Gostiny Dvor)

Taiga   FASHION & ACCESSORIES

19 🔒 Map p98, D1

Like several other of the city's trendy hang-outs, Taiga keeps a low profile despite its prime location close by the Hermitage. The warren of small rooms in the ancient building are worth exploring to find cool businesses ranging from a barber to fashion and books. (Тайга; http://taiga. space; Dvortsovaya nab 20; ⊙1-9pm; 🛜; Ⓜ Admiralteyskaya)

Au Pont Rouge   DEPARTMENT STORE

20 🔒 Map p98, B4

Dating from 1906–07 the one-time Esders and Scheefhaals department store has been beautifully restored and is one of the most glamorous places to shop in the city. This glorious Style Moderne building is now dubbed Au Pont Rouge after the **Krasny most** (Red Bridge) it stands beside. Inside you'll find choice fashions and accessories and top-notch souvenirs. (https://aupontrouge.ru; nab reki Moyki 73-79; ⊙10am-10pm; Ⓜ Admiralteyskaya)

Explore

Sennaya, Kolomna & Vasilyevsky Island

West of the Historic Heart, the city is characterised by the traditionally poor area around Sennaya pl (Haymarket) and the many waterways of Kolomna Island. Across the Neva lies vast, industrial Vasilyevsky Island (VO), with a concentration of historical sights at its eastern end.

The Sights in a Day

☀ Delve into an intriguing era of Russian history when you explore the lavish interiors of the **Yusupov Palace** (p116). Then fast forward into the 21st century to bask in the greenery and art-filled spaces on the island of **New Holland** (p118).

☀ Make your way across to Vasilyevsky Island, where once again you're presented with the contrast between past and present. **Kunstkamera** (p116) was Russia's first museum, set up by Peter to dispel common superstitions about illness and disease and includes an infamous collection of deformed foetuses preserved in bottles. From the fantastical to the fantastic, the **Erarta Museum of Contemporary Art** (p110) contains a superb collection of contemporary and Soviet underground art.

☽ In the evening, return to Kolomna to catch a show at the **Mariinsky Theatre** (p108).

For a local's day on Vasilyevsky Island (pictured left), see p112.

👁 Top Sights

Mariinsky Theatre (p108)

Erarta Museum of Contemporary Art (p110)

🔍 Local Life

Exploring Vasilyevsky Island (p112)

♥ Best of Sennaya, Kolomna & Vasilyevsky Island

Eating

EM Restaurant (p119)

Severyanin (p118)

Drinking

Beer Boutique 1516 (p120)

Entertainment

Mariinsky Theatre (p108)

Getting There

Ⓜ **Metro** Sennaya is served by the interconnecting Sennaya Pl (line 2), Spasskaya (line 4) and Sadovaya (line 5) stations. The most useful stations on Vasilyevsky Island are Vasileostrovskaya on line 3 and Sportivnaya on line 5. There are no metro stops in Kolomna.

🚌 **Bus** Bus 3 connects the Mariinsky with Nevsky pr, while trolleybus 5 connects pl Truda with Nevsky pr.

Top Sights
Mariinsky Theatre

The Mariinsky Theatre has played a pivotal role in Russian ballet ever since it was built in 1859 and remains one of Russia's most loved and respected cultural institutions. Its pretty green-and-white main building on aptly named Teatralnaya pl (Theatre Square) is a must for any visitor wanting to see one of the world's great ballet and opera stages.

Мариинский театр

⊙ Map p114, E5

☎ 812-326 4141

www.mariinsky.ru

Teatralnaya pl

⊙ box office 11am-7pm

Ⓜ Sadovaya

Exterior, Mariinsky II

Mariinsky I

The building you see today opened its doors in 1860, and was named in honour of Maria Alexandrovna, the wife of Tsar Alexander II. Since its inception, the Mariinsky has seen some of the world's greatest musicians, dancers and singers on its stage. Petipa choreographed his most famous works here, including *Swan Lake* and *The Nutcracker*, and the premieres of Tchaikovsky's *The Queen of Spades* and Prokofiev's *Romeo & Juliet* were also held here.

Mariinsky II

Finally opening its doors in 2013 after more than a decade of construction, legal wrangles, scandal and rumour, the **Mariinsky II** (Мариинский II; ul Dekabristov 34; tickets ₽350-6000) is a showpiece for St Petersburg's most famous ballet and opera company. It is one of the most technically advanced music venues in the world, with superb sightlines and acoustics from all of its 2000 seats. There's no denying that the modern-yet-not-modern-enough-to-be-interesting exterior is no great addition to St Petersburg's magnificent wealth of buildings. Inside, though, it's a different story. The interior is a beautifully crafted mixture of backlit onyx, multi-level public areas between which staircases, lifts and escalators weave, limestone walls, marble floors and Swarovski chandeliers.

Getting Tickets

Book ahead of time to see the ballet or opera performance you're interested in at the Mariinsky Theatre, especially during the White Nights, when performances of popular productions sell out months in advance. You can book and pay for tickets on the website, and then collect them at the box office before the performance, which is much better than trying to find what's available once you're in town.

☑ **Top Tips**

▶ It's easy to book tickets online; reserve well in advance in the busy summer months.

▶ Private tours are sometimes available – ask at the main ticket office if these are running during your visit.

▶ Be sure to dress the part. Russians don their finest for a night out at the Mariinsky.

✂ **Take a Break**

The Répa (p119) serves high-end fare in a stylish setting just behind the Mariinsky.

Elegant Sadko (p118) has dramatic flair and a wide-ranging menu.

Top Sights
Erarta Museum of Contemporary Art

Erarta's superb hoard of 2300 pieces of Russian contemporary art trumps its somewhat far-flung location. Housed in an ingeniously converted neoclassical Stalinist building, the museum is spread over five floors, with the main galleries focused on the permanent collection.

Музей современного искусства Эрарта

◉ Map p114, A4

www.erarta.com

29-ya Liniya 2

adult/under 21yr ₽500/350

🕙10am-10pm Wed-Mon

Ⓜ Vasileostrovskaya

Permanent Collection

The permanent collection is an excellent survey of the past half-century of Russian art. It's particularly strong on late-Soviet underground art. One nice curatorial touch is the frequent inclusion of objects depicted in paintings – a bowl of apples will sit, for example, in front of a painting entitled *Apple Picking*. It's all terribly sleek, beautifully presented and the best place in St Petersburg to get a feel for contemporary Russian art.

Temporary Exhibits

A new wing has significantly expanded the space for temporary exhibitions. One unusual feature is the inclusion of commercial galleries, where the work on display is also for sale. These tend to feature contemporary installations, paintings, video art and sculpture by Russian artists, and are worth checking out.

Extras

There are also installation spaces, occasional shows, plus a good restaurant and gift shop. Consider trying out at least one of eight 'U Space Total Installations', (₽200 for up to five people), small themed rooms that immerse you in worlds ranging from childhood to outer space. An extra ticket (₽250) is also required for the Theatre With No Actors, a sound-and-vision show on the 2nd floor.

Getting There

From Vasileostrovskaya metro station, catch bus 6 or 7, or trolleybus 10 or 11 from the opposite side of the road.

☑ Top Tips

▶ Call ahead to book very good tours in English (₽2200 for a group of up to 20; museum tickets must also be bought).

▶ Kids will love the cartoon screenings featuring famous works of art come to life on the 3rd floor.

▶ Check online for details of concerts, plays, lectures, film screenings and other creative events that take place on the stage here.

✗ Take a Break

If you want a drink and snack then head to the **Coffee Rooms** on the museum's 3rd floor.

For a more substantial meal, including creatively designed desserts, head to **Restaurant Erarta** (Ресторан Erarta; ☎ 812-334 6896; http://erartacafe.com; mains ₽510-810; ⊘ noon-11pm Mon-Sat, until 10pm Sun) on the museum's ground floor.

Local Life
Exploring Vasilyevsky Island

The eastern edge of Vasilyevsky Island was originally designed to be the administrative heart of the city under Peter the Great. The plan was never carried out, but it's still crammed with classical buildings housing institutions, excellent museums, and the sprawling campus of St Petersburg State University.

1 **Panoramic View**

The eastern nose of Vasilyevsky Island, the **Strelka** (Birzhevaya pl; **M**Vasileostrovskaya), boasts an unparalleled panorama, looking out over the Peter and Paul Fortress, the Hermitage, the Admiralty and St Isaac's Cathedral. The red **Rostral Columns** (Ростральная колонна) frame the view; climb the steps of the **Old Stock Exchange** for a raised perspective.

❷ Bureaucratic Beginnings

At Peter's behest, Domenico Trezzini built the magnificent **Twelve Colleges** (Двенадцать коллегий; Mendeleevskaya liniya), now St Petersburg State University, in 1722. The emperor based his bureaucracy here: separate entrances for each ministry signified their independence, while the unified facade highlighted collective goals. Now it's part of the university, and you'll find here the small **Mendeleev Museum** (Музей-Архив Санкт-Петербургского Университета Д.И.Менделеева; 812-328 9744; Universitetskaya nab 7-9; admission free; 11am-4pm Mon-Fri), the beautiful university botanical gardens and a quirky collection of sculptures.

❸ Petrine Palace

Peter originally gifted the entirety of Vasilyevsky Island to his best friend, Prince Menshikov, who proceeded to build the fabulous **Menshikov Palace** (Государственный Эрмитаж-Дворец Меншикова; 812-323 1112; www.hermitagemuseum.org; Universitetskaya nab 15; admission ₽300; 10.30am-6pm Tue, Thu, Sat & Sun, to 9pm Wed & Fri) on the north bank of the Bolshaya Neva. Menshikov's humble origins gave him a taste for opulence, and the interior is the best-preserved Petrine decor in the city.

❹ Artistic Institutions

Two Egyptian sphinx monuments mark the entrance to the institutional **Academy of Arts Museum** (Музей Академии Художеств; 812-323 6496; www.nimrah.ru; Universitetskaya nab 17; ₽500, photos ₽500; noon-8pm Wed, 11am-7pm Thu, Sat & Sun, 1-9pm Fri), which houses 250 years' worth of artistic expression. On display are works created by academy students and faculty over the years, as well as temporary exhibitions. A beautiful old library – lined with dusty volumes and packed with dark wood furniture – is open for visiting researchers.

❺ Medicine Man

Pop into the **Pharmacy Museum of Dr Pelya** (Аптека Доктора Пеля; 812-328 1628; http://aptekapelya.ru; 7-ya liniya 16-18; admission free; 9am-10pm) to view the good doctor's original 19th-century interior. The building still houses a doctors' clinic; it has a beautifully preserved facade as well as the original pharmacy on the ground floor.

❻ Baroque Beauty

Across Bolshoy pr, the street is pedestrianised and tree-lined, with the charming **St Andrew's Cathedral** (Андреевский собор; 812-323 3418; http://andrew-sobor.ru/; 6-ya liniya 11) on the corner. Completed in 1786, this baroque-style cathedral is a handsome feature of Vasilyevsky Island's skyline.

❼ Street Smart

Hang with the locals on 6-ya and 7-ya liniya, the main pedestrian and commercial street of Vasilyevsky Island. Lined with cafes, bars, restaurants and shops, this is a great place to grab a bite to eat before checking out the modern art at the **Novy Museum** (Новый музей; 812-323 5090; www.novymuseum.ru; 6-ya liniya 29; adult/student ₽200/100; noon-7pm Wed-Sun).

Smolensky most

Smolenka River

nab reki Smolenki

Kamskaya ul

12-13 linii

19 🔒

Maly pr

🎯16
Sportivnaya

4-ya liniya i 5-ya liniya

2-ya liniya i 3-ya

6-ya liniya i 7-ya liniya

8-9 linii

Smolenskoe Cemetery

10-ya liniya i 11-ya liniya

🎯15

Sredny pr

VASILEVSKY ISLAND

Maly pr

12-ya liniya i 13-ya liniya

14-ya liniya i 15-ya liniya

16-ya liniya i 17-ya liniya

8-ya liniya i 9-ya liniya

Ⓜ Vasileostrovska

18-ya liniya i 19-ya liniya

20-ya liniya i 21-ya liniya

22-ya liniya i 23-ya liniya

24-ya liniya i 25-ya liniya

Klubny per

Bolshoy pr

Sredny pr

Vasileostrovets Gardens

Erarta Museum of Contemporary Art
👁

Detskaya ul

Bolshoy pr

nab Leytenanta Shmidta

Bolshaya Neva

MARIINSKY

Khrapovitsky mos

nab Masanogo kanala

26-27 linyi

Matisov most

nab reki Pryazhki

Angliysky pr

Matisov

ul A Bloka

ul Dekabris

For reviews see	
👁 Top Sights	p108
◉ Sights	p116
✖ Eating	p117
🍷 Drinking	p120
★ Entertainment	p120
🔒 Shopping	p121

N

0 _____ 500 m
0 _____ 0.25 miles

E

F

G

H

shkov
st

**PETROGRAD
SIDE**

Peter & Paul
Fortress

1

Malaya Neva

Neva

9 ✕

nab Makarova

*Birzhevoy
most*

Neva

Volkhovsky per

Dvortsovaya nab

linya i Kadetskaya linya

Mendeleevskaya linya

Central Naval Museum
(Old Stock Exchange)
Birzhevaya pl

Millionnaya ul

2

Repina

University
Botanical
Gardens

Kunstkamera

12 ✕ 3

St Petersburg
State
University

*Dvortsovy
most*

Winter
Palace

Universitetskaya nab

Dvortsovaya pl
(Palace Square)

General
Staff
Building

nab reki Moyki

3

ul Repina

Angliyskaya nab

Admiralty

Admiralteysky proezd

Nevsky pr

agoveshchensky
most

Alexander
Garden

Admiralteysky pr

M
Admiralteyskaya

Zelyony
most

liyskaya nab

Galernaya ul

St Isaac's
Cathedral

Krasny
most

nab reki Moyki

Kazanskaya ul

4

ernaya ul

MARIINSKY

Central
Naval
Museum

Konnogvardeysky bul

ul Yakubovicha

Pochtamtskaya ul

7 ✕

Moyka

Gorokhovaya ul

2 ◎

ul Truda

Bolshaya Morskaya ul

nab reki Moyki

per Antonenko

ew Holland
Island

Yusupov
Palace

13 ✕

per Pirogova

Voznesensky pr

KAZANSKY

11 ✕

Grivtsova pr

Sadovaya ul

*Gorokhovaya
ul*

1 ◎

17 ⓘ

ul Dekabristov

Grazhdanskaya ul

20 🔒

Matveevsky
most

10 ✕

*Lviny
most*

nab kanala Griboedova

8 ✕

Sadovaya

M
Sadovaya

M
**Sennaya
Pl**

6

5 ✕

ul Glinki

18 ★

Stolyarny
per

ul Yefimova

Sadovaya

Mariinsky ◎
Theatre

14 ✕

SENNAYA

M
Spasskaya

5

KOLOMNA

4 ◎

Sights

Yusupov Palace
PALACE

1 ⊙ Map p114, F4

This spectacular palace on the Moyka River has some of best 19th-century interiors in the city, in addition to a fascinating and gruesome history. The palace's last owner was the eccentric Prince Felix Yusupov, a high-society darling and at one time the richest man in Russia. Most notoriously, the palace is the place where Grigory Rasputin was murdered in 1916, and the basement where this now infamous plot unravelled can be visited as part of a guided tour. (Юсуповский дворец; ☎921-970 3038; www.yusupov-palace.ru; nab reki Moyki 94; adult/student incl audio guide ₽700/500, Rasputin tour ₽350/250; ⊙11am-6pm; Ⓜ Sadovaya)

Central Naval Museum
MUSEUM

2 ⊙ Map p114, E4

Following a move to this beautifully repurposed building opposite the former shipyard of New Holland, the Central Naval Museum has moved into the 21st century and is now one of St Petersburg's best history museums. The superb, light-bathed building houses an enormous collection of models, paintings and other artefacts from three centuries of Russian naval history, including *botik,* the small boat known as the 'grandfather of the Russian navy' – stumbling across it in the late 17th century was Peter the Great's inspiration to create a Russian maritime force. (Центральный военно-морской музей; ☎812-303 8513; www.navalmuseum.ru; pl Truda; adult/student ₽600/400; ⊙11am-6pm Wed-Sun; Ⓜ Admiralteyskaya)

Kunstkamera
MUSEUM

3 ⊙ Map p114, F2

Also known as the Museum of Ethnology and Anthropology, this is the city's first museum, founded in 1714 by Peter himself. It is famous largely for its ghoulish collection of monstrosities, preserved 'freaks', two-headed mutant foetuses, deformed animals and odd body parts, all collected by Peter. While most rush to see these sad specimens, there are also interesting exhibitions on native peoples from around the world. (Кунсткамера; ☎812-328 1412; www.kunstkamera.ru; Universitetskaya nab 3, entrance on Tamozhenny per; adult/child ₽300/100; ⊙11am-7pm Tue-Sun; Ⓜ Admiralteyskaya)

Piter Kayak
KAYAKING

4 ⊙ Map p114, F5

Experienced kayaker Denis and his friendly young team lead these excellent early morning tours which last around four hours and cover 11km. The canals and rivers are at their quietest at this time and, unlike on regular boat tours, the slower pace allows you to admire the wonderful surroundings at leisure. (☎921-435 9457; http://piterkayak.com; nab Kryukova kanala 26; tours ₽1700-R2500; ⊙tours at 7am Tue-Sun Apr-Sep)

Interior, Yusupov Palace

Eating

1818 Kafe and Bikes
INTERNATIONAL $

5  Map p114, E5

Combining a love of bicycles and street food from around the globe, Kafe and Bikes serves up delicious cooking amid upbeat grooves, exposed bulbs and those slate grey walls so prevalent in SPB. Shawarmas, wok-fried buckwheat noodles with vegetables, pizzas, *khachapuri* (Georgian cheese bread) and *syriniki* are all served up in a hurry by friendly staff. (Кафе и Велосипеды; www.cafe1818.ru; ul Dekabristov 31; mains ₽240-420; ⊙10am-11pm Mon-Fri, from 11am Sat & Sun; 🛜🚲; MSadovaya)

Co-op Garage
PIZZA $

6  Map p114, H5

Tucked into an unmarked courtyard off Gorokhovaya, this sprawling restaurant and drinking den is the go-to spot for creatively topped thin-crust pizzas and craft beers. The industrial setting draws a chatty crowd of tatted-up hipsters and style mavens, with a mostly rock soundtrack playing in the background. On warm days you can take a table in the courtyard. (www.cooperativegarage.com; Gorokhovaya 47; pizzas ₽260-390; ⊙noon-midnight Sun-Thu, to 2am Fri & Sat; 🛜🚲)

Local Life
New Holland

The triangular island **New Holland** (Map 114, E4; Новая Голландия; www.new hollandsp.ru; nab Admiralteyskogo kanala; ⏰9am-10pm Mon-Thu, to 11pm Fri-Sun; Ⓜ️Sadovaya) was closed for the most part of the last three centuries, and has opened to the public in dazzling fashion. There's plenty going on, with hundreds of events happening throughout the year. There are summertime concerts, art exhibitions, yoga classes and film screenings, plus restaurants, cafes and shops. You can also come to enjoy a bit of quiet on the grass – or on one of the pontoons floating in the pond.

Teplo
MODERN EUROPEAN $$

 7 Map p114, F4

This much-feted, eclectic and original restaurant has got it all just right. The venue itself is a lot of fun to nose around, with multiple small rooms, nooks and crannies. Service is friendly and fast (when it's not too busy) and the peppy, inventive Italian-leaning menu has something for everyone. Reservations are usually required, so call ahead. (📞812-570 1974; www.v-teple. ru; Bolshaya Morskaya ul 45; mains ₽360-940; ⏰9am-midnight Mon-Fri, from 11am Sat & Sun; ❄🛜🌿; Ⓜ️Admiralteyskaya)

Severyanin
RUSSIAN $$

8 Map p114, G5

An old-fashioned elegance prevails at Severyanin, one of the top choices for Russian cuisine near Sennaya pl. Amid vintage wallpaper, mirrored armoires and tasseled lampshades, you might feel like you've stepped back a few decades. Start off with the excellent mushroom soup or borsch, before moving on to rabbit ragout in puff pastry or Baltic flounder. (Северянин; 📞921-951 6396; www.severyanin.me; Stolyarny per 18; mains ₽620-1300; ⏰noon-midnight; 🛜; Ⓜ️Sennaya Ploshchad)

Buter Brodsky
EUROPEAN $$

 9 Map p114, E1

This chic cafe-bar dedicated to poet Joseph Brodsky (the name is a pun on the Russian word for sandwich, *buter-brod*) is a super-stylish addition to Vasilyevsky Island's eating and drinking scene. The menu runs from excellent *smørrebrød* (open sandwiches; from ₽260) to various set meals of salads and soup. (Бутер Бродский; 📞8-911-922 2606; https://vk.com/buterbrodskybar; nab Makarova 16; mains ₽260-780; ⏰noon-midnight; 🛜; Ⓜ️Sportivnaya)

Sadko
RUSSIAN $$

 10 Map p114, F5

Serving all the Russian favourites, this impressive restaurant's decor combines traditional Zhostovo floral designs and Murano glass chandeliers amid vaulted ceilings and elegantly set tables. It's popular with theatregoers (reserve ahead in the high season), as it's an obvious pre- or post-Mariinsky dining option. (📞812-903 2373; www.sadko-rst.ru; ul Glinki 2; mains ₽540-1200; ⏰noon-1am; 🧒; Ⓜ️Sennaya Ploshchad)

Julia Child Bistro
INTERNATIONAL $

11 Map p114, G5

This neighbourhood charmer is a fine anytime spot, with good coffees, teas and snacks, plus creative thoughtfully prepared dishes such as *kasha* (porridge) with mushrooms and feta for breakfast, or halibut with lemon cabbage and celery mousse later in the day. Kindly staff and a laid-back setting will make you want to stick around for a while. (812-929 0797; Grazhdanskaya ul 27; mains ₽310-490; 9am-11pm Mon-Fri, from 10am Sat & Sun; M Sadovaya)

Restoran
RUSSIAN $$$

12 Map p114, F2

Nearly 20 years on the scene and this excellent place is still going strong. Stylish and airily bright, Restoran is somehow formal and relaxed at the same time. The menu combines the best of *haute-russe* cuisine with enough modern flair to keep things interesting: try duck baked with apples or whole baked sterlet (a species of sturgeon) in white wine and herbs. (Ресторанъ; 812-323 3031; Tamozhenny per 2; mains ₽700-2600; noon-11pm; M Admiralteyskaya)

EM Restaurant
EUROPEAN $$$

13 Map p114, F4

Bookings are essential for this superb restaurant where the chefs calmly prepare seven beautifully presented courses in an open kitchen. Be prepared for such exotic elements as reindeer, smoked perch, red cabbage sorbet and foie gras coloured with squid ink. Individual food preferences can be catered to and every Sunday they work their culinary magic on a vegan menu. (921-960 2177; http://emrestaurant.ru; nab reki Moyki 84; set menu ₽3500; 7-11pm Tue-Sun; M Admiralteyskaya)

The Répa
RUSSIAN $$$

14 Map p114, F5

Repa may be Russian for turnip but this delightful restaurant, cheek-by-jowl with the Mariinsky, is anything but rustic. Beautifully painted murals of dancers grace the walls as waiters glide by delivering glasses of sparkling wine and plates of bliny, *kamchatka* crab or whole baked fish to elegantly attired customers. (812-640 1616; http://ginza.ru/spb/restaurant/therepa; Teatralnaya pl 18/10; mains ₽370-1490; 5pm-1am Mon-Fri, 2pm-1am Sat & Sun; M Sadovaya)

☑ Top Tip

Bridges

If you're staying (or drinking) on Vasilyevsky Island, remember that in the summer months the bridges go up at night. Dvortsovy most's timetable is up at 1.10am and down for 20 minutes at 2.50am before going up again until 4.55am. Blagoveshchensky most is crossable from 2.45am until 3.10am and then not again until 5am.

Drinking

Beer Boutique 1516　CRAFT BEER

15　Map p114, D2

Your craft-beer cravings are sure to be satisfied at this bar and bottle shop that has dedicated itself to the best of local and international ales. There's usually around 17 beers on tap and 300 or so in bottles to choose from – so it could be a long night. (Пивной бутик 1516; ☎812-328 6066; http://butik1516.ru; 9-ya liniya 55; ⏰3-10pm; Ⓜ Vasileostrovskaya)

Radosti Kofe　CAFE

16　Map p114, D1

A leafy, relaxed ambience and river views across to the Petrograd side make this a pleasant pit stop for coffee, other drinks and snacks while touring Vasilyevsky Island. They can make their drinks with soy, almond or hazelnut milk as well. The menu is available in English. (Радости Кофе; ☎812-925 7222; www.facebook.com/radosticoffee/; nab Makarova 28; ⏰8am-11pm; 🛜; Ⓜ Sportivnaya)

Solaris Lab　CAFE

17　Map p114, F5

Set inside a glass, semi-spherical dome, Solaris Lab has magnificent views over the russet rooftops of St Petersburg to the glittering dome of St Isaac's. It draws a mixed crowd of families and hipsters, who linger over pots of high-quality tea and tasty desserts (try the lemon tart). On warm days, there's outdoor seating on the rooftop. (www.facebook.com/solarislab11; per Pirogova 18, 4th fl; ⏰1pm-midnight; Ⓜ Sadovaya)

Entertainment

Rimsky-Korsakov Conservatory　CLASSICAL MUSIC

18　Map p114, F5

This illustrious music school was the first public music school in Russia. The Bolshoy Zal (Big Hall) on the 3rd floor is an excellent place to see performances by up-and-coming musicians throughout the academic year, while the Maly Zal (Small Hall) often hosts free concerts from present students and alumni; check when you're in town for what's on. (Консерватория имени Н. А. Римского-Корсакова; ☎812-312 2519; www.conservatory.ru; Teatralnaya pl 3; tickets ₽300-2000; Ⓜ Sadovaya)

Dining at Sadko (p118)

Shopping

Artmuza ARTS & CRAFTS

19 Map p114, B1

This is one of the city's largest 'creative clusters' with around 13,000 sq metres of space over several floors hosting a variety of art galleries, studios, fashion boutiques and designers. On the ground floor look out for the joint atelier of Snega Gallery and Slavutnitsa where designers specialise in making clothes and accessories based on traditional Russian costumes and patterns. (Артмуза; ☎812-313 4703; http://artmuza. spb.ru; 13-ya liniya 70-72; ⊘11am-10pm; M Sportivnaya)

Rediska ARTS & CRAFTS

20 Map p114, G5

Near the courtyard of the Berthold Centre, this delightful shop has lots of eye-catching objects, much of it made in-house or produced by St Petersburg artisans. You'll find jewellery imprinted with famous paintings, whimsical wooden clocks, ceramics, tiny Konstructor kits (a kind of miniature Lego), artfully painted flasks, backpacks, sunglasses and handmade soaps, lotions and candles. (Grazhdanskaya ul 13, Berthold Centre; ⊘noon-10pm; M Sadovaya)

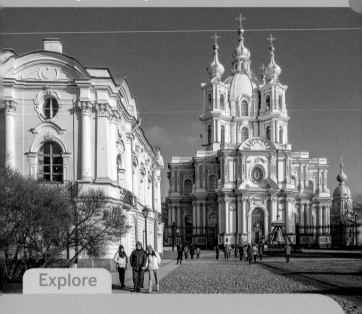

Smolny & Vosstaniya

The Smolny peninsula is a well-heeled residential district dominated by the Smolny Cathedral (pictured above). South of Nevsky
pr, Vosstaniya is the focus of St Petersburg's underground art and
drinking scene, while Vladimirskaya is a mercantile district full of
shopping, markets and a clutch of quirky museums.

The Sights in a Day

☀ Start your day at the historic **Alexander Nevsky Monastery** (p124), where you can spend a few hours exploring the holy grounds and locating the gravestones of Russia's cultural icons.

☀ Take a quick metro ride into the heart of the Lieyny district, where there's much to discover on neighbourhood wanders – from browsing record stores and indie booksellers on streets south of Nevsky to cafe-hopping on restaurant-lined ul Rubinshteyna. While you're in the neighbourhood, make the obligatory bibliophile stop at the **Dostoevsky Museum** (p128) or experience contemporary Russian culture at **Loft Project ETAGI** (p128).

☾ By night, the district has just as much to offer, with some of the best bars in the city, particularly around the Liteyny area. Catch some jazz at **Hat** (p132), sip cocktails at **Dead Poets Bar** (p132) or sample the local craft beers at **Redrum** (p132).

◉ Top Sights

Alexander Nevsky Monastery (p124)

♥ Best of Smolny & Vosstaniya

Eating
Duo Gastrobar (p129)

Banshiki (p130)

Drinking
Redrum (p132)

Dead Poets Bar (p132)

Griboyedov (p132)

Dyuni (p133)

Soviet History
Museum of the Defence & Blockade of Leningrad (p128)

Contemporary Art
Loft Project ETAGI (p128)

Getting There

Ⓜ **Metro** Accessed by Ploschad Vosstaniya/Mayakovskaya, Vladimirskaya/Dostoevskaya, Ploschad Alexandra Nevskogo, Chernyshevskaya and Ligovsky Prospekt.

🚌 **Bus** Handy for getting up or down Nevsky pr in minutes, dozens of buses and trolleybuses run this route, including buses 24 and 191, which run the entirety of Nevsky.

Top Sights
Alexander Nevsky Monastery

Named after the patron saint of St Petersburg who led the Russian victory over the Swedes in 1240, the Alexander Nevsky Monastery is the city's oldest and most eminent religious institution. Today it is a working monastery that attracts scores of devout believers, as well as being the burial place of some of Russia's most famous artistic figures.

Александро-Невская лавра

◉ Map p126, E6

www.lavra.spb.ru

Nevsky pr 179/2

cemetery ₽400, pantheon ₽150

⏲ grounds 6am-11pm summer, 8am-9pm winter, churches 6am-9pm, cemeteries 9.30am-6pm summer, 11am-4pm winter, pantheon 11am-5pm Tue, Wed & Fri-Sun

Ⓜ Ploshchad Aleksandra Nevskogo

Cemeteries

Coming into the monastery complex, you'll first arrive at the opposing cemeteries, which hold the remains of some of Russia's most famous names. You'll find Dostoevsky, Tchaikovsky, Rimsky-Korsakov, Borodin and Mussorgsky within the walls of the **Necropolis of Art Masters** (Некрополь Мастеров Искусств; www.gmgs.ru; incl Necropolis of the 18th Century ₽400; ☻9.30am-6pm May-Sep, 11am-4pm Oct-Apr), which is on your right after you enter the monastery's main gate. Across the way in the **Necropolis of the 18th Century** (Некрополь XVIII века; incl Necropolis of Art Masters ₽400; ☻9.30am-6pm May-Sep, 11am-4pm Oct-Apr), you'll find far more graves, though fewer famous names – look out for polymath Mikhail Lomonosov and Natalya Lanskaya (Pushkin's wife) as well as the graves of the St Petersburg architects Quarenghi, Stasov and Rossi.

Monastery

The monastery itself is within a further wall beyond the cemeteries. The centrepiece is the classical **Holy Trinity Alexander Nevsky Lavra** (Свято-Троицкая Александро-Невская Лавра; ☻6am-9pm;), which was built between 1776 and 1790. Hundreds crowd in here on 12 September to celebrate the feast of St Alexander Nevsky, whose remains are in the silver reliquary by the elaborate main iconostasis, which you'll find to the right of the main alter, under a red and gold canopy. Behind the cathedral is the **Nikolsky Cemetery** (admission free; ☻9.30am-6pm May-Sep, 11am-4pm Oct-Apr), a beautiful spot with a little stream running through it, where more recently deceased Petersburgers can be found, including former mayor Anatoly Sobchak and murdered Duma deputy Galina Starovoytova.

☑ Top Tips

▶ You can wander for free around most of the grounds, but you need tickets to enter the two cemeteries and the Blagoveshchenskaya Burial Vault.

▶ The route to the Nikolsky Cemetery is not signed. Take one of the passages on either side of Trinity Cathedral's main entrance – marked with туалет (toilet) signs.

▶ At the Blagoveshchenskaya Burial Vault, info in English is available on a small touchscreen in the corner.

✗ Take a Break

The monastery's on-site **canteen** (open 9am to 7pm) has snacks, as well as inexpensive cafeteria-style lunch fare from 1pm to 2pm.

For sandwiches, pastas and snacks, **Bien Cafe & Bar** (Nevsky pr 166; mains ₽340-480; ☻8am-11pm Mon-Fri, from 10am Sat & Sun; Ⓜ Pl Alexandra Nevskogo) is a 10-minute walk up Nevsky pr.

Stavropolskaya ul

Tverskaya ul

Kavalergardskaya ul

ul Kirochnaya

Suvorovsky pr

ul Kirochnaya

Degtyarny per

ul Moiseenko

Novgorodskaya ul

Kirovskaya ul

Shpalernaya ul

Tauride Palace

ul Tavricheskaya

Tavricheskaya ul

SMOLNY

9-ya Sovetskaya ul

8-ya Sovetskaya ul

7-ya Sovetskaya ul

6-ya Sovetskaya ul

5-ya Sovetskaya ul

Vodoprovodny per

Robespiera

Tauride Gardens

Kirochnaya ul

ul Paradnaya

Potyomkinskaya ul

13 ❌

Vilensky per

Ozerny per

12 ❌

Lirovsky pr

Grechesky pr

Neva

nab Robespiera

pr Chernyshevskogo

Chernyshevskaya Ⓜ

ul Radishcheva

ul Vosstaniya

ul Nekrasova

ul Vosstaniya

Shpalernaya ul

Zakharevskaya ul

ul Chaykovskogo

Furshtatskaya ul

Kirochnaya ul

6 ❌
7 ❌

ul Ryleeva

Sapyorny per

Baskov per

16 ❌

Kovensky per

ul Mayakovskogo

ul Zhukovskogo

nab Kutuzova

Shpalernaya ul

5 ❌

ul Korolenko

9 ❌

ul Chekhova

17 ❌

Nevsky

Mokhovaya ul

Gagarinskaya ul

1 ⓘ

Museum of the Defence & Blockade of Leningrad

ul Pestelya

LITEYNY

Liteyny pr

14 ⓖ

4 ⓖ

Anna Akhmatova Museum at the Fountain House

admiralty pr

Anichkov most

15 ⓖ

nab reki Fontanki

Fontanka

nab reki Fontanki

2 ⓜ

3

Nevsky pr

pl Ostrovskogo

4

nab reki Fontanki

Neva

Sinopskaya nab

Nikolsky
Cemetery

Lazarus
Cemetery

VOSSTANIYA

Tikhvin
Cemetery

Pl Alexandra
Nevskogo

Ispolkomskaya ul

Alexander Nevsky
Monastery

Alexander
Nevsky
Gardens

nab Obvodnogo kanala

ul Bakunina

Perekupnoy per

Konnaya ul

ul Myasnaya

ul Myrtnis

Nevsky pr

Telezhnaya ul

Mirgorodskaya ul

Obvodny Canal

Kremenchugskaya ul

Pl Vosstaniya

Moscow Station
(Moskovsky
Vokzal)

Dneproetrovskaya ul

Ligovsky pr

18

19

VOSSTANIYA

2 Loft Project
ETAGI

Transportny per

Ligovsky
Prospekt

Romenskaya ul

Pavlogradsky
per

VLADIMIRSKAYA

ul Marata

Dostoevsky
Museum

3

Kolomenskaya ul

ulRazyezzhaya

Voronezhskaya ul

Ligovsky pr

Dostoevskaya

Vladimirskaya

ul Pravdy

ul Dostoevskogo

Borovaya ul

nab Obvodnogo kanala

ul Rubinshte

ul Lomonosova

Zagorodny pr

ul Marata

ul Razvezzhaya

Zvenigorodskayaul

10

5

6

7

8

For reviews see	
⊙ Top Sights	p124
⊙ Sights	p128
⊗ Eating	p129
⊕ Drinking	p132

500 m
0.25 miles

N

0
0

Sights

Museum of the Defence & Blockade of Leningrad   MUSEUM

1 Map p126, A2

The grim but engrossing displays here contain donations from survivors, propaganda posters from the blockade period and many photos depicting life and death during the siege. You'll see the meagre bread rations as they dwindled by the month, drawings made by children trying to cope with the loss of family members, and snapshots taken during Shostakovich's *Symphony Number 9* – composed and played during the siege (by famished musicians), to show the world that Leningrad was not down for the count. (Музей обороны и блокады Ленинграда; www.blokadamus. ru; Solyarnoy per 9; ₽250, audio guide ₽300; ☺10am-6pm Thu-Mon, 12.30-8.30pm Wed; MChernyshevskaya)

Loft Project ETAGI   CULTURAL CENTRE

2 Map p126, B6

This fantastic conversion of the former Smolninsky Bread Factory has plenty to keep you interested, including many of the original factory fittings seamlessly merged with the thoroughly contemporary design. A young creative crowd flock to the mazelike space that includes galleries and exhibition spaces, eye-catching shops, a hostel, a bar and a cafe with a great summer terrace all spread out over five floors. In the yard, converted shipping containers house yet more pop-up clothing shops, record sellers, cafes and eateries whipping up creative street food. (Лофт проект ЭТАЖИ; ☏812-458 5005; www.loftprojectetagi.ru; Ligovsky pr 74; rooftop ₽100; ☺9am-11pm; MLigovsky Prospekt)

Dostoevsky Museum   MUSEUM

3 Map p126, B5

Fyodor Dostoevsky lived in flats all over the city, mostly in Sennaya, but his final residence is this 'memorial flat' where he lived from 1878 until he died in 1881. The apartment remains as it was when the Dostoevsky family lived here, including the study where he wrote *The Brothers Karamazov,* and the office of Anna Grigorievna, his wife, who recopied, edited and sold all of his books. (Литературно-мемориальный музей Ф.М. Достоевского; www.md.spb.ru; Kuznechny per 5/2; adult/student ₽250/100, audio guide ₽250; ☺11am-6pm Tue & Thu-Sun, 1-8pm Wed; MVladimirskaya)

Anna Akhmatova Museum at the Fountain House   MUSEUM

4 Map p126, A4

Housed in the south wing of the Sheremetyev Palace, this touching and fascinating literary museum celebrates the life and work of Anna Akhmatova, St Petersburg's most famous 20th-century poet. Akhmatova lived here from 1926 until 1952, invited by the art scholar Nikolai

Khachapuri po-adzharski (Georgian cheese bread with raw egg)

Punin, who lived in several rooms with his family. The two had a long-running affair, somewhat complicated by the tight living situation – Punin didn't want to separate from his wife. (Музей Анны Ахматовой в Фонтанном Доме; www.akhmatova.spb.ru; Liteyny pr 51; adult/child ₽120/free, audio guide ₽200; ☉10.30am-6.30pm Tue & Thu-Sun, noon-8pm Wed; MMayakovskaya)

Eating

Duo Gastrobar   FUSION $

 Map p126, B2

Boasting a minimalist Scandinavian design scheme, Duo Gastrobar has

wowed diners with its outstanding cooking that showcases quality ingredients with global accents in delectable plates such as crab bruschetta, duck breast with smoked cheese and tomato, and rich French onion soup. There's an excellent wine list (more than a dozen by the glass) as well. (☎812-994 5443; www.duobar.ru; ul Kirochnaya 8A; mains ₽350-500; ☉1pm-midnight; MChernyshevskaya)

Khachapuri i Vino   GEORGIAN $

 Map p126, B2

This welcoming, warmly lit space serves outstanding Georgian fare. The recipes aren't overly complicated, and the fine ingredients speak for

Local Life

Bekitzer

Always crowded and spilling out into the street, **Bekitzer** (Map p126, A5; Бекицер; 812-926 4342; www.facebook.com/bktzr; ul Rubinshteyna 40; mains ₽180-450; ⊘noon-6am Mon-Fri, from noon Sat & Sun; 🛜🖊; MDostoyevskaya) is an Israel-themed eatery and drinking den, luring hip and joyful people with its creative cocktails, Israeli Shiraz and the best falafel wraps this side of the Baltic sea.

themselves in flavour-rich dishes such as aubergine baked with *suluguni* (a type of cheese), pork dumplings, and tender lamb stew with coriander. Don't miss the excellent *khachapuri* (cheese bread), which comes in a dozen varieties and is whipped up by the bakers in the front. (📞812-273 6797; Mayokovskogo 56; mains ₽310-390; ⊘noon-midnight; 🛜🖊; MChernyshevskaya)

Schengen   INTERNATIONAL $$

7 Map p126, B2

A breath of fresh air just off Liteyny pr, Schengen represents local aspirations to the wider world. The wide-ranging menu is packed with temptations, from tender halibut with tomatoes and zucchini to slow-cooked venison with parsnip cream and plums in red wine. It's served up in a cool and relaxing two-room space where efficient staff glide from table to table. (Шенген; 📞812-922 1197; ul Kirochnaya 5; mains ₽480-850; ⊘9am-

midnight Mon-Fri, from 11am Sat & Sun; 🛜; MChernyshevskaya)

Banshiki   RUSSIAN $$

8 Map p126, C5

Although it opened in 2017, Banshiki has already earned a sterling reputation for its excellent Russian cuisine, serving up a huge variety of nostalgic dishes with a contemporary touch. Everything is made in-house, from its refreshing *kvas* to dried meats and eight types of smoked fish. Don't overlook cherry *vareniki* (dumplings) with sour cream, oxtail ragout or the rich borsch. (Банщики; 📞921-941 1744; www.banshiki.spb.ru; Degtyanaya 1; mains ₽500-1100; ⊘11am-11pm; 🛜; MPloschad Vosstaniya)

Vsyo na Svyom Mestye   INTERNATIONAL $$

9 Map p126, B2

A hip little gastrobar with a warm ambience, tables made of converted sewing machines and a record player providing the tunes. Stop in for creative market-fresh fare, which might include cod filet on cauliflower purée, ramen soup, or polenta with roast chicken and oyster mushrooms – all goes nicely with the craft brews and easygoing vibe. (Всё на Своём Месте; 📞812-932 0256; Liteyny pr 7; mains ₽380-740; ⊘noon-midnight)

Taste to Eat   RUSSIAN $$

10 🍴 Map p126, A5

This popular, handsomely designed restaurant along the Fontanka River serves up quality ingredients from across Russia in innovative dishes including smoked mackerel paté, orzo with crab from Kamchatka, and curry with lamb stewed in *kvas*. With its sun-filled big windows, comfy leather seating and good wine list, it makes a fine setting for a leisurely meal, day or night. (Вкус Есть; ☎812-983 3376; http://tastetoeat. tastetoeat.ru; nab reki Fontanki 82; mains ₽480-680; ⏱1-11pm; ☎)

Geografiya INTERNATIONAL $$

 Map p126, A4

True to its name, this hip little place takes diners on a culinary journey around the globe, with a standout menu of Singapore-style noodles with seafood, Szechuan beef with jasmine rice and Thai coconut soup, plus plenty of Russian classics (try the homemade dumplings). (География; ☎812-340 0074; www.geo-rest.com; ul Rubinshteyna 5; ₽450-700; ⏱noon-midnight; ☎⏚; Ⓜ Mayakovskaya)

Mechta Molokhovets RUSSIAN $$$

 Map p126, C3

Inspired by the cookbook of Elena Molokhovets, the menu at 'Molokhovets' Dream' covers all the classics from borsch to beef stroganoff, as well as less frequently seen dishes such as venison tenderloin with juniper sauce or wild mushrooms with sour cream and pickled onions. Whatever you have here, you can be sure it's the definitive version.

(Мечта Молоховец; ☎812-929 2247; www.molokhovets.ru; ul Radishcheva 10; mains ₽950-2200; ⏱noon-11pm; ❄☎; Ⓜ Ploshchad Vosstaniya)

Blok STEAK $$$

 Map p126, C2

On the top floor of the Leningrad Centre, Blok aims to dazzle with big, bold artworks, a sculptural chandelier running down the glass-covered ceiling, and two terraces with sweeping skyline views. None of this detracts from the star of the show: perfectly grilled steak, which comes in 23 varieties – including *muromets*, a tender perfection that is dry-aged in-house. (Блок; ☎812-415 4040; www.blok.restaurant; Potyomkinskaya ul 4; mains ₽750-5800; ⏱noon-1am; ☎; Ⓜ Chernyshevskaya)

Ⓠ Local Life
Ziferblat

A charming multi-room 'free space' that has started a worldwide trend, **Ziferblat** (Map p126, C4; Циферблат; ☎981-180 7022; www.ziferblat.net; 2nd fl, Nevsky pr 81; per min ₽3, per min after 1st hr ₽2; ⏱11am-midnight; ☎; Ⓜ Ploshchad Vosstaniya) is the original anti-cafe in St Petersburg. Coffee, tea, soft drinks and biscuits are included as you while away your time playing chess and other board games, reading, playing instruments (help yourself to the piano and guitar) or just hanging out with the arty young locals who frequent its cosy rooms.

Drinking

Hat
BAR

14 Map p126, A3

The wonderfully retro-feeling Hat is a serious spot for jazz and whiskey lovers, who come for the nightly live music and the cool cat crowd who makes this wonderfully designed bar feel like it's been transported out of 1950s Greenwich Village. A very welcome change of gear for St Petersburg's drinking options, but it can be extremely full at weekends. (ul Belinskogo 9; ⏰7pm-5am; Ⓜ Gostiny Dvor)

Commode
BAR

15 Map p126, A4

Stopping in for drinks at Commode feels more like hanging out in an upper-class friend's stylish apartment. After getting buzzed up, you can hang out in various high-ceilinged rooms, catch a small concert or poetry slam, browse books in the quasi-library, play a round of table football, or chat with the easygoing crowd who have fallen for the place. (www.commode.club; ul Rubinshteyna 1, 2nd fl; per hr ₽180; ⏰4pm-2am Sun-Thu, to 6am Fri & Sat)

Redrum
BAR

16 Map p126, B3

One of St Petersburg's best drinking dens, Redrum hits all the right notes. It has a cosy, white-brick interior, a welcoming, easygoing crowd, and a stellar line-up of craft brews (some two dozen on tap). There's also good pub fare on hand to go with that creative line-up of Session IPAs, Berliner Weisse and porters. (☎812-416 1126; www.facebook.com/redrumbarspb; ul Nekrasova 26; ⏰4pm-1am Sun-Thu, to 3am Fri & Sat; Ⓜ Mayakovskaya)

Dead Poets Bar
COCKTAIL BAR

17 Map p126, B3

This very cool place has a sophisticated drinks menu and an almost unbelievable range of spirits stacked along the long bar and served up by a committed staff of mixologists. It's more of a quiet place, with low lighting, a jazz soundtrack and plenty of space to sit down. (☎812-449 4656; www.deadpoetsbar.com; ul Zhukovskogo 12; ⏰2pm-2am Sun-Thu, to 8am Fri & Sat; 🛜; Ⓜ Mayakovskaya)

Local Life
Griboyedov

This is hands-down the longest-standing and most respected music **club** (Map p126,B7; Грибоедов; www.griboedovclub.ru; Voronezhskaya ul 2a; ⏰noon-6am Mon-Fri, from 2pm Sat & Sun; 🛜; Ⓜ Ligovsky Prospekt) in the city. A repurposed bomb shelter, this one was founded by local ska collective Dva Samolyota. It's a low-key bar in the early evening, gradually morphing into a dance club later in the night. Admission varies from free to upwards of ₽400, depending on who's playing or spinning.

Museum of the Defence & Blockade of Leningrad (p128)

Dyuni
BAR

18 Map p126, C6

What looks like a small suburban house sits rather incongruously here amid repurposed warehouses in this vast courtyard. There's a cosy indoor bar and a sand-covered outside area with table football and ping pong, which keeps the cool kids happy all night in the summer months. To find it, simply continue 300m in a straight line from the courtyard entrance on Ligovksy pr. (Дюны; www.facebook.com/dunes.on.ligovsky; Ligovsky pr 50; noon-3am Sun-Thu, to 6am Fri & Sat; M Ploshchad Vosstaniya)

Fish Fabrique Nouvelle
LIVE MUSIC

19 Map p126, B5

This legendary bar is set in the building that's the focus of the avant-garde art scene – it attracts an interesting crowd who give this cramped space its edge. Live bands kick up a storm most nights around 10pm. (www.fishfabrique.spb.ru; Ligovsky pr 53; 3pm-late; M Ploshchad Vosstaniya)

Explore

Petrograd
& Vyborg Sides

The Petrograd Side is a fascinating place that includes the Peter & Paul Fortress and an impressive clutch of Style Moderne buildings lining its main drag. The Vyborg Side is famous for its role in Soviet history; a walk around the fascinating post-industrial landscape will appeal to travellers with palace fatigue.

The Sights in a Day

☼ The area's showstopper of a sight is the **Peter & Paul Fortress** (p136). Spend the morning exploring the founding site of St Petersburg, including the museums, soaring cathedral and panoramic views. Afterwards, stroll up the main thoroughfare of Bolshoy pr, which is dotted with shops, restaurants and intriguing architecture.

☼ After lunch take your pick from the excellent museums that dot the district – the post-industrial **Street Art Museum** (p142); the fascinating **Hermitage Storage Facility** (p142); and the fantastically detailed **Museum of Political History** (p142). Except for the last one, the museums are far-flung, so you probably have to choose just one.

☾ Venues for eating, drinking and entertainment are sparse in these outlying areas. But you can't go wrong with dinner at **Chekhov** (p144) or **Staraya Derevnya** (p144), both of which promise classic, satisfying Russian fare in a delightful setting.

For a local's day in Chkalovskaya, see p138.

 Top Sights

Peter & Paul Fortress (p136)

 Local Life

Discover Chkalovskaya (p138)

 Best of Petrograd & Vyborg Sides

Eating
Staraya Derevnya (p144)

Koryushka (p144)

Drinking
Big Wine Freaks (p145)

Entertainment
Kamchatka (p145)

Getting There

Ⓜ **Metro** Line 2 serves the Petrograd Side at Gorkovskaya and Petrogradskaya stations, while line 5 does the same at Sportivnaya, Chkalovskaya and Krestovsky Ostrov.

🚌 **Bus** Bus 10 runs from the Vyborg Side at Chyornaya Rechka, down Bolshoy pr on the Petrograd Side and into the Historic Heart. *Marshrutka* (fixed route minibus) 346 runs the length of Bolshoy pr and continues on to the Vyborg Side.

🚊 **Tram** Trams 6 and 40 also traverse the Petrograd Side.

Top Sights
Peter & Paul Fortress

Housing a cathedral, a former prison and various exhibitions, this large defensive fortress on Zayachy Island is the kernel from which St Petersburg grew into the city it is today.

Having captured this formerly Swedish settlement on the Neva, Peter set to turn the outpost into a modern Western city, starting with the Peter & Paul Fortress in 1703. It has never been utilised in the city's defence – unless you count incarceration of political 'criminals' as national defence.

Петропавловская крепость

◉ Map p140, D5

www.spbmuseum.ru

grounds free, SS Peter & Paul Cathedral adult/child ₽450/250, combined ticket for 5 exhibitions ₽600/350

🕒 grounds 8.30am-8pm, exhibitions 11am-6pm Mon & Thu-Sun, 10am-5pm Tu

Ⓜ Gorkovskaya

Fortress Walls

A separate ticket gains you access to both the Postern, a 97.4m passage hidden in the fortress walls, and the **Neva Panorama** (adult/student ₽300/270; ⏱10am-8pm Thu-Tue), a walkway atop the walls which concludes at Naryshkin Bastion. At noon every day a cannon is fired from here, a tradition dating back to Peter the Great's times.

SS Peter & Paul Cathedral

All of Russia's prerevolutionary rulers from Peter the Great onwards (except Peter II and Ivan VI) are buried in the magnificent baroque interior of this **cathedral** (adult/student ₽450/250; ⏱10am-7pm Mon, Tue & Thu-Sat, 11am-7pm Sun). From May to October you can climb the landmark needle-thin spire of the **bell tower** (adult/child ₽250/150).

Commandant's House

The fascinating museum in the **Commandant's House** (adult/student ₽200/120; ⏱11am-6pm Mon & Thu-Sun, to 5pm Tue) charts the history of the St Petersburg region from medieval times to 1918. What starts as a fairly standard-issue plod through the city's history really comes alive upstairs, with modern, interactive exhibits (even though there's still a lack of explanations in English).

Trubetskoy Bastion

Trubetskoy Bastion (adult/student ₽200/120; ⏱10am-7pm Thu-Mon, to 6pm Tue) is the best of the fort's exhibits, thanks to the evocative use of the original cells for displays about former political prisoners, including the likes of Maxim Gorky, Leon Trotsky, Mikhail Bakunin and Fyodor Dostoevsky. Short biographies in English of the various inmates are posted on the doors.

☑ **Top Tips**

▶ Go at opening time and head straight to SS Peter & Paul Cathedral to beat the worst of the crowds.

▶ While some sights can be skipped, you shouldn't miss the Commandant's House, which gives an excellent historical overview of St Petersburg.

▶ For the complete story, hire an audio guide, which has loads of details on the fortress and what lies within.

✗ **Take a Break**

Within the fortress grounds, you can grab a snack at the *stolovaya* **Leningradskoye Kafe** (mains ₽240-360; ⏱10am-8pm Thu-Tue).

A far nicer option is Koryushka (p144), at the southwestern end of Zayachy Island.

Local Life
Discover Chkalovskaya

A few metro stops north of the historic centre, Chkalovskaya is an up-and-coming Petrograd Side area with architectural treasures, enticing cafes, and some intriguing art on the streets. With its mix of Soviet monuments and glittering new storefronts, this mash-up of old and new makes a fascinating place for a wander.

❶ Art & Airplanes

The neighbourhood takes its name from Valery Chkalov (1904–38), the legendary aircraft test pilot who pioneered the polar air route from Russia to North America. The **metro station** pays homage to this airman with its biplane-like design and emblems that evoke propellers. In front of the station is a small statue of Chkalov.

2 Style Moderne Gem

The Style Moderne gem **Leuchtenberg House** (Bolshaya Zelenina ul 28) is so called because it once belonged to the Duke of Leuchtenberg, great-grandson of Tsar Nicholas I. Cross the street to take in the full glory of the mosaic frieze spread across the upper story of the facade, the key decorative feature of the architect Theodor von Postels.

3 Lunch Break

For a peek inside the building, head to the ground-floor **Paninaro** (Bolshaya Zelenina 28; mains ₽380-780; ⏰9am-11.30pm Mon-Fri, from 11am Sat & Sun; 🖊), a laid-back Italian restaurant and cafe. The exposed brick walls and old-fashioned tile floors make a fine setting for house-made pastas topped with grilled vegetables, creative salads and pizzas, and refreshing cocktails.

4 From Constructivism to Street Art

Over on Pionerskaya ul, the **Red Banner Textile Factory** (Трикотажная фабрика "Красное Знамя"; Pionerskaya ul 53; admission free) is a grand relic of Soviet constructivist architecture. Street artists have commandeered walls around the abandoned industrial space to create an outdoor gallery of technicolour images, mainly along Korpusnaya ul.

5 Soviet Heroes

Continuing along Pionerskaya ul, you'll find a **monument** (Pionerskaya ul 39) dating from the Soviet period. Busts of five children's heads are carved in high relief-style next to a description that reads: 'Honor and glory to the children of Petersburg workers who perished in October 1917'. The location was used as an artillery post by the Red Guard to fire onto a military school nearby. A handful of boys helped bring shells to the site.

6 Sweet Ending

Across the street from the mural, you'll find the **Bulochnye F Volcheka** (Булочные Ф. Вольчека; Pionerskaya ul 35; pastries ₽30-60; ⏰8am-10pm; 🛜), which whips up tasty pastries and baked goods including croissants, eclairs and berry-covered tarts. You can grab a seat at the window and take in the view of the mural (just visible under the bakery's awnings), while enjoying a cappuccino and something sweet.

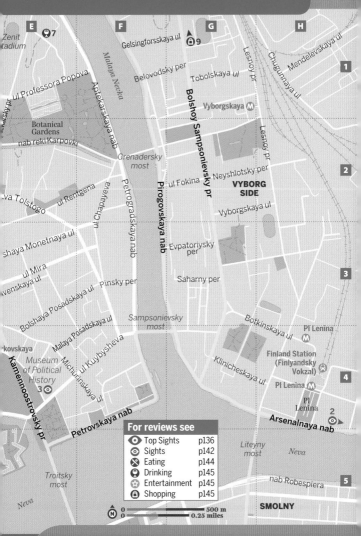

Zenit Stadium

7

Professora Popova

ul Professora Popova

Botanical Gardens

nab reki Karpovki

va Tolstogo

ul Rentgena

shaya Monetnaya ul

ul Mira

ivenskaya ul

Bolshaya Posadskaya ul

Malaya Posadskaya ul

kovskaya

Museum of Political History 3

kamennoostrovsky pr

Michurinskaya ul

ul Kuybysheva

F

Malaya Nevka

Aptekarskaya nab

Grenadersky most

Petrogradskaya nab

Pirogovskaya nab

ul Chapayeva

Bolshaya Posadskaya ul

Pinsky per

Sampsonievsky most

Petrovskaya nab

Troitsky most

Neva

Gelsingforsskaya ul

9

Belovodsky per

Bolshoy Sampsonievsky pr

ul Fokina

Evpatoriysky per

Saharny per

G

Tobolskaya ul

Vyborgskaya M

Neyshlotsky per

VYBORG SIDE

Vyborgskaya ul

Botkinskaya ul

Klinicheskaya ul

Pl Lenina M

Finland Station (Finlyandsky Vokzal)

Pl Lenina M

Pl Lenina

2

Arsenalnaya nab

Liteyny most

Neva

nab Robespiera

SMOLNY

H

Lesnoy pr

Chugunnaya ul

Mendelevskaya ul

Lesnoy pr

1

2

3

4

5

For reviews see

◉	Top Sights	p136
◎	Sights	p142
✕	Eating	p144
🍷	Drinking	p145
★	Entertainment	p145
🔒	Shopping	p145

N 0 ___ 500 m
0 ___ 0.25 miles

Sights

Hermitage Storage Facility

MUSEUM

1 🎯 Map p140, C1

Guided tours of the Hermitage's state-of-the-art restoration and storage facility are highly recommended. This is not a formal exhibition as such, but the guides are knowledgeable and the examples chosen for display (paintings, furniture and carriages) are wonderful.The storage facility is directly behind the big shopping centre opposite the metro station – look for the enormous golden-yellow glass facility decorated with shapes inspired by petroglyphs. (Реставрационно-хранительский центр Старая деревня; 📞812-340 1026; www.

hermitagemuseum.org; Zausadebnaya ul 37a; tours ₽550; ⏱tours 11am, 1pm, 1.30pm & 3.30pm Wed-Sun; 🚹; Ⓜ Staraya Derevnya)

Street Art Museum

GALLERY

2 🎯 Map p140, H4

It's well worth the effort making the trip out to see this magnificent collection of street art set inside an 11-hectare, former industrial site. You'll find a wide variety of formats, from huge murals covering walls to mixed-media installations set inside a former boilerhouse. Every year, the exhibition changes, with top artists from around the globe invited to contribute on themes such as Revolution (featured in 2017 on the 100-year anniversary of Russia's October Revolution), Migrants and Peace. (📞812-448 1593; http://streetartmuseum.ru; shosse Revolutsii 84, Okhta, entrance on Umansky per; adult/student ₽350/250; ⏱noon-10pm Tue-Sun May-Sep; Ⓜ Ploshchad Lenina, then bus 28, 37, 137 or 530)

Museum of Political History

MUSEUM

3 🎯 Map p140, E4

The elegant Style Moderne Kshesinskaya Palace (1904) is a highly appropriate location for this excellent museum – one of the city's best – covering Russian politics in scrupulous detail up to contemporary times. The palace, previously the home of Mathilda Kshesinskaya, famous ballet dancer and one-time lover of Nicholas II in his pre-tsar days, was briefly the

---

🔍 Local Life

Kirovsky Islands

This is the collective name for the three outer delta islands of the Petrograd Side – **Kamenny** (Map p140, A1; Каменный остров; Ⓜ Chyornaya Rechka), **Yelagin** (Ⓜ Krestovsky Ostrov) and **Krestovsky** (Map p140, A1; Крестовский остров; Ⓜ Krestovsky Ostrov). Once marshy forests, the islands were granted to 18th- and 19th-century court favourites and developed into elegant playgrounds. Still mostly parkland, they are leafy venues for picnics, river sports and White Nights' cavorting, as well as home to St Petersburg's super rich.

Understand
St Petersburg Goes Style Moderne

Industrialisation during the latter part of the 19th century brought huge wealth to St Petersburg, which resulted in an explosion of commissions for major public buildings and mansions, many in the much-feted style of the time – art nouveau, known in Russia as Style Moderne.

In the Historic Heart area, you only have to walk down Nevsky Prospekt (past the State Hermitage Museum) to see several of the key results of this daring architectural departure: the **Singer Building** (Map p98, D3; Nevsky pr 28; Ⓜ Nevsky Prospekt) and **Kupetz Eliseevs** (Map p98, G4; p104), both of which have been restored to their full glory in recent years, are ostentatious in their decorative details. Also in the historic heart, search out Au Pont Rouge (p105), a revival of the old department store Esders and Scheefhaals, which combines Moderne and Italianate features, and **DLT** ((Map p98, B4; ДЛТ; ☎ 812-648 0848; www.dlt.ru; Bolshaya Konyushennaya ul 21-23; ⏰ 10am-10pm; Ⓜ Nevsky Prospekt), finished in 1909 as the department store for the elite Petersburg Guards regiments, and still operating as the city's most luxurious fashion house. The romantic interior of the Vitebsk Station (Vitebsky vokzal), crafted at the turn of the 19th century, offers up stained glass, sweeping staircases and beautiful wall paintings in its spacious waiting halls.

But it is over on the Petrograd Side, the most fashionable district of the era, that the majority of Style Moderne buildings can be found. Highlights include the Troitsky Bridge, the fabulous mansion of the ballet dancer Mathilda Kshesinskaya, now the Museum of Political History (p142), and much of Kamennoostrovsky pr, which is lined with prime examples. Poke around the district's back streets to discover many gems from the early 20th century, including **Chaev Mansion** (Map p140, E2; ul Rentgena 9; ⏰ 8am-2pm & 3-9pm Mon-Fri, 9am-2pm Sat; Ⓜ Petrogradskaya) and Leuchtenberg House (Map p140, A2; p139).

headquarters of the Bolsheviks, and Lenin often gave speeches from the balcony. (Музей политической истории России; ☏812-313 6163; www.polithistory.ru; ul Kuybysheva 4; adult/child ₽200/free, audio guide ₽200; ◷10am-6pm Sat-Tue, 10am-8pm Wed & Fri, closed Thu; Ⓜ Gorkovskaya)

Eating

Chekhov

RUSSIAN $$

 4 Map p140, D2

Despite a totally nondescript appearance from the street, this restaurant's charming interior perfectly recalls that of a 19th-century dacha (summer country house) and makes wonderful setting for a meal. The

menu, hidden inside classic novels, features lovingly prepared dishes such as roasted venison with bilberry sauce or Murmansk sole with dill potatoes and stewed leeks. (Чехов; ☏812-234 4511; http://restaurant-chekhov.ru; Petropavlovskaya ul 4; mains ₽550-890; ◷noon-11pm; Ⓜ Petrogradskaya)

Lev y Ptichka

GEORGIAN $$

 5 Map p140, B4

Amid big fur hats, a lion (*lev*) mural, decorative wooden chandeliers and other curious design elements, this friendly spot has a loyal local following for its delicious and reasonably priced Georgian fare, including piping hot *khachapuri* (Georgian cheese bread) fired up at the baker's oven in front. Plates are small and meant for sharing. Entrance is on ul Chaykino. (Лев и Птичка; ☏988-7069; Bolshoy pr 19; 🛜 🍴)

Koryushka

RUSSIAN, GEORGIAN $$

 6 Map p140, D5

Lightly battered and fried smelt (*koryushka*) is a St Petersburg speciality every April, but you can eat the small fish year-round at this relaxed, sophisticated restaurant beside the Peter & Paul Fortress. There are plenty of other very appealing Georgian dishes on the menu to supplement the stunning views across the Neva. (Корюшка; ☏812-640 1616; www.ginza.ru/spb/restaurant/korushka; Petropavlovskaya krepost 3, Zayachy Island; mains ₽650-2400; ◷noon-1am; 🛜 🚼; Ⓜ Gorkovskaya)

Drinking

Big Wine Freaks
WINE BAR

7 Map p140, E1

Boasting a stylish contemporary design, this aptly named place serves an excellent variety of wines from Europe and the New World, plus tasty snacks to go with those tempranillos and chardonnays. Helpful staff – all trained sommeliers – can provide ordering tips. There's live music, along the lines of acoustic jazz, on Wednesday nights from 8pm. (📞921-938 6063; Instrumentalnaya ul 3; ⊙6pm-1am Tue-Sat; 🛜)

Entertainment

Kamchatka
CLUB, LIVE MUSIC

8 Map p140, C4

A shrine to Viktor Tsoy, the late Soviet-era rocker who worked as caretaker of this former boilerhouse bunker with band mates from Kino. Music lovers flock here to light candles and watch a new generation thrash out their stuff. The line-up is varied and it's worth dropping by if only for a quick drink in this highly atmospheric place – find it tucked in a courtyard off the street. (www.clubkamchatka.ru; ul Blokhina 15; cover ₽250-350; ⊙7pm-2am; Ⓜ Sportivnaya)

Shopping

Udelnaya Fair
MARKET

9 🔒 Map p140, G1

This treasure trove of Soviet ephemera, pre-revolutionary antiques, WWII artefacts and bonkers kitsch from all eras is truly worth travelling for. Exit the metro station to the right and follow the crowds across the train tracks. Continue beyond the large permanent market, which is of very little interest, until you come to a huge area of independent stalls, all varying in quality and content. (Удельная ярмарка; Skobolvesky pr, Vyborg Side; ⊙8am-5pm Sat & Sun; Ⓜ Udelnaya)

Local Life
The Soviet South

Sprawling southern St Petersburg was once planned to be the centre of Stalin's Leningrad, and it contains grand buildings, over-the-top monuments and sculpture-lined green spaces that celebrate now mostly forgotten figures of the past. You'll also see largely middle-class Russians and families, who've given new life to these marble-lined boulevards.

Getting There

Ⓜ Take the blue line to Moskovskoe Vorota Station. From there you can walk the entire route, though you can also use the metro to break up some of the longer stretches.

1 Moscow Triumphal Arch

Bristling with spears, shields and banners, this imposing 12-columned gate was built to celebrate victory in the 1828 Russo-Turkish War and once marked the southern entrance to the imperial capital. In 1936 the gates were dismantled under Stalin's order and were later used as anti-tank defences in WWII. They were restored in 1960.

2 Grand Maket Rossiya

Russia in all its grit and glory – from the industrial sprawl of Magnitogorsk to the glittering domes of Moscow – is on full display at this vast **re-creation of the motherland in miniature** (☎812-495 5465; www.grandmaket.ru; Tsvetochnaya ul 16; adult/child ₽480/280, audio guide or binoculars ₽250; ⊙10am-8pm; Ⓜ Moskovskoe Vorota). One huge room contains mountains, cities, rivers and lakes, with lots of mechanised action that you can observe while strolling around.

3 Park Pobedy

This large green space gathers a cross-section of Petersburgers, including young families, teens and canoodling couples who stroll the leafy paths and enjoy the views over the ponds and flower gardens. Built to celebrate Russia's victory in WWII, the **park** (Moskovsky pr; ⊙6am-midnight; Ⓜ Park Pobedy) is full of statues of Soviet war heroes, and has a beneficent depiction of Lenin interacting with small children.

4 Chesme Church

This striking red-and-white, 18th-century, Gothic **church** (Чесменская церковь; https://chesma.spb.ru; ul Lensoveta 12; ⊙10am-7pm; Ⓜ Moskovskaya) commemorates the 1770 Battle of Chesme. This is where Catherine the Great was standing when news arrived of the victory over the Turks. The capricious monarch ordered a shrine be built to preserve this historic moment. It now seems particularly incongruous with its Stalinist surroundings.

5 House of Soviets

Begun by Noi Trotsky in 1936, the bombastic **House of Soviets** (Дом советов; Moskovsky pr 212; Ⓜ Moskovskaya) was only finished after the war, by which time the architect had been purged. Nonetheless, this magnificently sinister building is a great example of Stalinist design, with its columns and bas-reliefs and an enormous frieze across the top.

6 Monument to the Heroic Defenders of Leningrad

Centred around a 48m-high obelisk, the **monument** (Монумент героическим защитникам Ленинграда; www.spbmuseum.ru; pl Pobedy; ₽200; ⊙10am-6pm Thu-Mon, until 5pm Tue; Ⓜ Moskovskaya), unveiled in 1975, symbolises the city's encirclement and eventual victory in WWII. On a lower level, flickering torches ring a very moving sculpture depicting the city's suffering. From there, you can enter an underground exhibition, which delves into the war and siege.

The Best of
Moscow &
St Petersburg

Moscow & St Petersburg's Best Walks

Moscow Metro:
Underground Art................ 150

St Petersburg's
Historic Heart 152

Moscow & St Petersburg's Best...

Museums & Galleries 154

Imperial History................. 156

Soviet History.................... 157

Contemporary Art................ 158

Architecture 159

Tours 160

Eating 162

Drinking & Nightlife 164

Entertainment................... 166

For Free......................... 168

For Kids 170

Shopping........................ 172

Church of the Saviour on the Spilled Blood (p96), St Petersburg
MARINA ZEZELINA/SHUTTERSTOCK ©

Best Walks
Moscow Metro: Underground Art

The Walk

Every day, as many as seven million people ride the Moscow metro. What's more, this transport system marries function and form: many of the stations are marble-faced, frescoed, gilded works of art. Take this tour for an overview of Moscow's most interesting and impressive metro stations. The best time to take a tour is Saturday or Sunday morning or any evening after 8pm. The price is ₽55.

Start Ⓜ Komsomolskaya

End Ⓜ Park Pobedy

Distance 18km; one to two hours

Take a Break

There are plenty of excellent options around Triumfalnaya pl (Ⓜ Mayakovskaya) and along Kamergersky per (Ⓜ Teatralnaya).

Interior, Komsomolskaya metro stationn

❶ Komsomolskaya

The intersecting stations are both named for the youth workers who helped with early construction. In the line-one station, look for the Komsomol emblem at the top of the limestone pillars and the majolica-tile panel showing the volunteers hard at work.

From Komsomolskaya, proceed anti-clockwise around the Ring line, getting off at each stop along the way.

❷ Belorusskaya

The ceiling mosaics celebrate the culture, economy and history of Russia's neighbour to the west. The 12 ceiling panels illustrate different aspects of their culture, while the floor pattern reproduces traditional Belarusian ornamentation. Switch here to line two (the green Zamoskvoretskaya line), where the Belarusian theme continues, and travel south.

❸ Mayakovskaya

The grand-prize winner at the 1938 World's Fair in New York, Mayakovskaya station has an art-deco central hall that's all pink rhodonite, with slender, steel columns. The inspiring looking mosaics on the ceiling depict *24 Hours in the Land of the Soviets*. This deep station (33m) served as an air-raid shelter during WWII.

❹ Teatralnaya

This station's decor follows a theatrical theme. The porcelain figures represent seven of the Soviet republics by wearing national dress and playing musical instruments from their homeland. Change here

to Ploshchad Revolyutsii station on line three (the dark-blue Arbatsko-Pokrovskaya line).

❺ Ploshchad Revolyutsii

This dramatic station is basically an underground sculpture gallery. The life-sized bronze statues represent the roles played by the people during the revolution and in the 'new world' that comes after. Heading up the escalators, the themes are revolution, industry, agriculture, hunting, education, sport and child rearing.

Touch the nose of the border guard's dog for good luck. Take line three heading west.

❻ Park Pobedy

This newer station opened after the complex at Poklonnaya Gora, which commemorated the 50th anniversary of the victory in the Great Patriotic War. It is the deepest Moscow metro station, and it has the longest escalators in the world. The enamel panels at either end of the hall depict the victories of 1812 and 1945.

Best Walks
St Petersburg's Historic Heart

🏃 The Walk

The historic heart of St Petersburg is World Heritage–listed for good reason: the city is a treasure trove of architectural masterpieces and superb museums. Follow this walking tour to see some of the highlights, starting with the dazzling ensemble that surrounds Palace Square. From this incomparable starting place, the route passes the city's most esteemed cultural institutions and its most elaborate churches. You'll experience eclectic architectural styles, historic bridges and lovely parks, ending at the city's central spine Nevsky Prospekt – an attraction in its own right.

Start Dvortsovaya pl; Ⓜ Admiralteyskaya

End Pl Ostrovskogo; Ⓜ Gostiny Dvor

Length 2km; three hours

🍴 Take a Break

Kupetz Eliseevs (p104)

Singer Building

❶ Palace Square

Approaching Palace Square (p100) from Bolshaya Morskaya ul, behold the Alexander Column, perfectly framed under the triumphal arch with the Winter Palace (p90) as its elaborate backdrop. Turn right at the square's northeast corner to find the colossal Atlantes holding aloft the portico of the New Hermitage.

❷ Death of a Poet

Along the Moyka River is the final residence of Russia's most celebrated poet – now the Pushkin Flat-Museum. Around the corner Konyushennaya pl is dominated by the 18th-century court stables, currently under restoration. In the middle of the complex you can visit the Church of the Saviour not Made by Human Hand where Pushkin's funeral service was held.

❸ Green Places & Sacred Spaces

Rest for a while in either the shady canalside Mikhailovsky Gardens. Revived, you'll now be ready for the spectacular

Church of the Saviour on the Spilled Blood (p96). There's a spectacular view of the church from Teatralny, near the intersection of the Moyka and Griboyedov Canal.

❹ Art Square

Detour off nab kanal Griboyedova to find a statue of Pushkin in the middle of pretty pl Iskusstv. The square is ringed by celebrated cultural institutions, including the Russian Museum (p100) and Mikhailovsky Theatre (p104).

❺ Architectural Landmarks

At the junction of Nevsky pr and nab kanal Griboyedova, admire the Russian Style Moderne beauty Singer Building. It's a whimsical contrast to the formidable Kazan Cathedral opposite. Behind the mammoth church, Bankovsky most is the city's most picturesque and photographed bridge.

❻ Ploshchad Ostrovskogo

The centrepiece of this small park is an enormous statue of Catherine the Great (1873), standing amid the chess, backgammon and mah-jong players who crowd the benches. At the Empress' heels are renowned statesmen of the 19th century, including her lovers Orlov, Potemkin and Suvorov. Enjoy the view of the impressive facade of the Alexandrinsky Theatre (p104).

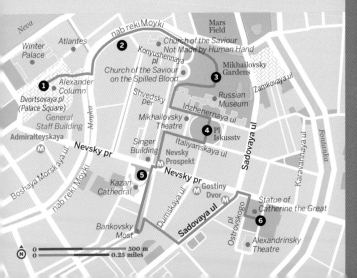

Best
Museums
& Galleries

POPOVA VALERIYA/SHUTTERSTOCK ©

Rich histories and dynamic culture are highlights of these cosmopolitan cities, as showcased by the ever-expanding array of museums and galleries. Once a cornerstone of conservatism, these venues are now experimenting with new technologies and subject matter, in an attempt to entertain and educate.

Fortress Museums

Both Moscow and St Petersburg were founded as fortresses, which still stand today as testament to (or in spite of) their humble beginnings.

Art Museums

Moscow and St Petersburg are home to celebrated, world-class art museums, with different institutions dedicated to Russian and European art. They are all spectacular venues – well worth a day (or more) to admire their wide-ranging collections. In addition to these standard bearers, both cities contain countless smaller niche galleries dedicated to particular artists or genres.

The Best of the Rest

History museums remember every era of Russia's past; countless country estates are now architectural museums; military museums commemorate the nation's wartime heroics; and anybody who was anybody has a 'house-museum' in their honour. There are space museums, Jewish museums, video-game museums; museums dedicated to chocolate, trains, vodka and more. Whatever you're into, Moscow or St Petersburg has a museum for you.

☑ **Top Tips**

▶ Most museums are closed at least one day a week – often Monday. Look for late evening hours at least one day a week (usually Thursday).

▶ Few museums have full signage in English. Audio guides in English are more common.

▶ Many museums still maintain a dual pricing system, whereby foreign visitors must pay a higher admission fee than Russian residents. Children, students and pensioners may receive discounts (even as foreigners).

Exhibit at the Armoury (p96), Kremlin, Moscow

Best Museums in Moscow

Armoury Russia's storehouse of priceless treasures and historic artefacts. (p26)

Pushkin Museum of Fine Arts A fantastic collection of European art in two buildings. (p56)

Tretyakov Gallery The crème de la crème of Russian art, from ancient icons to exquisite modernism. (p64)

Jewish Museum & Centre of Tolerance Genii and outcasts, dissidents and revolutionaries – the history of Jews in Russia at a glance. (p45)

Garage Museum of Contemporary Art Moscow's most cutting-edge museum. (p59)

Best Museums in St Petersburg

State Hermitage Museum Everybody's first-choice museum will not fail to amaze even the most jaded traveller. (p90)

Russian Museum Visiting the city's stellar collection of Russian art over the centuries is a sublime experience. (p100)

Erarta Museum of Contemporary Art Trek out to this excellent survey of Soviet underground and contemporary Russian art. (p110)

Fabergé Museum A must for anyone interested in late imperial Russian jewellery and decorative arts. (p100)

Best Literary Museums

Mikhail Bulgakov Museum The censored writer's former flat in Moscow offers a calendar of lively cultural events. (p44)

Tolstoy Estate-Museum See where Russia's most celebrated novelist lived and worked in Moscow. (p65)

Anna Akhmatova Museum at the Fountain House The unusual house-museum of St Petersburg's most famous modern poet is both tragic and uplifting. (p128)

Dostoevsky Museum This St Petersburg museum is a sufficiently suitable place to explore Dostoevsky's life. (p128)

Best
Imperial History

St Petersburg was Russia's imperial capital, as evidenced by the dozens of palaces scattered around the city. Throughout this period, Moscow retained its title of 'second capital' – and has a decent stash of period buildings and other artefacts to show for it.

DIMBAR76/SHUTTERSTOCK ©

Best Burial Sites

Archangel Cathedral
Moscow burial place of the Russian rulers from the 14th to the 17th centuries. (p26)

SS Peter & Paul Cathedral St Petersburg burial place of the Russian rulers from Peter I to Nicholas II. (p137)

Best Palaces in Moscow

Patriarch's Palace
Built for Patriarch Nikon mostly in the mid-17th century. (p25)

Armoury It's inside the Kremlin (not a palace), but it's a showcase for imperial excess, including jewels and dresses, crowns and carriages. (p26)

Best Palaces in St Petersburg

State Hermitage Museum Alongside the amazing art collection are the palace's fabulously decorated rooms. (p90)

Yusupov Palace The location of Rasputin's murder offers some of St Petersburg's best 19th-century interiors. (p116)

Menshikov Palace Beautiful Petrine interiors at this branch of the Hermitage on Vasilyevsky Island. (p113)

Best Day Trip

Grand Palace (www. peterhofmuseum.ru; ul Razvodnaya; adult/student ₽700/400, audio guide ₽600; ⏱10.30am-6pm Tue-Sun, closed last Tue of month) Hugging the Gulf of Finland, 29km west of St Petersburg, Peterhof – the 'Russian Versailles' – is a far cry from the original cabin Peter the Great had built here. Peter liked the place so much he built a villa, Monplaisir, here and then a whole series of palaces and ornate gardens. The palace and buildings are surrounded by leafy gardens and a spectacular ensemble of gravity-powered fountains.

Best
Soviet History

Seventy years of history is not soon forgotten – especially when they were years packed with construction, expansion, repression and dramatic cultural shifts. Nowadays, museums remember the best and worst of Soviet history, while relics from the period are integral parts of both cities' landscapes.

Best Historic Sites

Lenin's Mausoleum The founder of the Soviet state is still on display. (p29)

Moscow Metro An efficient transportation system in an incredible and ornate setting. (p150)

Art Muzeon A sculpture park where the heroes of the Soviet Union have been put out to pasture. (p64)

Palace Square Site of Bloody Sunday (1905) and the storming of the Winter Palace (1917). (p100)

Soviet South (p146) A walking tour of Soviet sights in St Petersburg. (p146)

Lubyanka The former headquarters of the KGB and the site of the notorious prison. (p78)

Best Soviet History Museums

Museum of Political History Housed in the elegant Kshesinskaya Palace, once the headquarters of the Bolsheviks. (p142)

Bunker-42 Cold War Museum Descend to the underground – literally – to see this secret Cold War bunker. (p78)

Gulag History Museum Stalin's slaughterhouse – the history of one of the world's cruellest prison systems. (p46)

Central Museum of the Armed Forces Covering the history of the Soviet and Russian military since 1917. (p45)

Museum of the Defense & Blockade of Leningrad A sobering and thorough account of the horrific 900-day blockade. (p128)

Museum of Soviet Arcade Machines Another side of Soviet history. (p44)

Best
Contemporary Art

The most intriguing aspect of Russia's contemporary art scene is not the established artists, but rather the up-and-coming creatives. See what they are up to at the post-industrial art centres that are popping up in both Moscow and St Petersburg.

(Self) Censorship

Artists now have tremendous freedom to depict all aspects of Russian life. Many art professionals state categorically that there is no censorship in Russia, although most acknowledge a degree of self-censorship. That said, anecdotal evidence shows that artists and curators risk prosecution, especially if they tackle such sensitive topics as the war in Chechnya or the Russian Orthodox Church.

Support for the Arts

In any case, contemporary art receives unprecedented support from the powers-that-be, with the government pitching in to fund prestigious events such as the **Moscow Biennale of Contemporary Art** (www.moscowbiennale.ru; ⏲ Sep). Many oligarchs have also stepped in to foster home-grown talent and develop a vibrant art scene. Leonid Mikhelson, Russia's richest man (according to Forbes), started the V-A-C Foundation to support contemporary art.

Best Contemporary Art in Moscow

Garage Museum of Contemporary Art Unusual, thought-provoking art in a ruined restaurant in Gorky Park. (p59)

Moscow Museum of Modern Art Hosts compelling rotating exhibits, especially at the branch outlets. (p44)

Winzavod A former wine-bottling facility now filled with art. (p74)

Best Contemporary Art in St Petersburg

Erarta Museum of Contemporary Art Though it only opened in 2010, Erarta has established itself as one of the world's best collections of modern and contemporary Russian art. (p110)

Street Art Museum An exciting new-concept museum based on the territory of a laminated plastics factory in the suburb of Okhta. (p142)

Loft Project ETAGI Once a bread factory, now an arts centre, packed with galleries, cafes and more. (p128)

Novy Museum Showcasing the 'nonconformist' artists from the Soviet period. (p113)

Best
Architecture

Nothing distinguishes the two Russian capitals more than their contrasting architectural styles. Moscow was the capital of ancient Rus, as demonstrated by its skyline of tent roofs and onion domes. St Petersburg was built as a 'window to the west,' and its landmarks reflect the influence of its Italian architects.

Moscow

Moscow's streets are a textbook of Russian history, with churches, mansions, theatres and hotels standing as testament to the most definitive periods, from medieval Byzantine to Moscow baroque to Russian revival. Despite the tendency to demolish and rebuild, Moscow has preserved an impressive array of architectural gems.

St Petersburg

Peter the Great's intention was to build a city that rivalled Paris and Rome for architectural splendour. He envisioned grand avenues, weaving waterways and magnificent palaces. His successors carried out their own even more elaborate versions of their forebear's plan. Today, the city's historic centre is a veritable museum of 18th- and 19th-century architecture, with enough baroque, neoclassical and empire-style extravagances to keep you ogling.

PROTASOV AN/SHUTTERSTOCK ©

Cathedral of Christ the Saviour Inspired by Byzantine Russian architecture. (p64)

Best Style Moderne

Museum of Political History Formerly the fabulous mansion of the ballet dancer Mathilda Kshesinskaya. (p142)

Kupetz Eliseevs This decorative delight has recently been restored to its fully glory. (p104)

Best Soviet Architecture

Narkomfin This constructivist landmark is undergoing a much-needed restoration. (p41)

Melnikov House The architect lived in this cylindrical house near the Arbat. (p61)

Best Baroque

Twelve Colleges A prime example of Petrine Baroque, created by Trezzini. (p113)

Winter Palace Rastrelli's masterpiece. (p91)

Best Russian Revival

State History Museum Inspired by medieval styles (interiors and exterior). (p32)

Best
Tours

Moscow and St Petersburg are big, overwhelming cities with a strange alphabet. Letting the locals show you around is a good way to get your bearings and learn something new. It also gives you a chance to chat up a real, live Russian and perhaps make a friend.

Best Moscow Walking Tours

Moscow 360 (☎8-985-447 8688; www.moscow360.org; tours per group from ₽2000) Paul is a private guide who offers excellent and entertaining walking tours in the centre. His speciality is the AK-47 tour, which takes you to a shooting range to learn all about the infamous AK weapons and take a few shots yourself.

Moscow ArchiGeek (Москва Глазами Инженера; ☎499-322 2325; www.archigeek.ru; tours from ₽1200) These architectural tours around Moscow hit some unusual destinations.

Patriarshy Dom Tours (☎495-795 0927; www.toursinrussia.com; Moscow School No 1239, Vspolny per 6; Moscow tours from US$22, day trips from US$65; Ⓜ Barrikadnaya) Provides a changing schedule of specialised tours of local museums, specific neighbourhoods and unusual themes.

Moscow Greeter (www.moscowgreeter.ru; admission free) Let a local volunteer show you what they love about their city! Every tour is different, as the volunteer decides (perhaps with your input) where to go.

Moscow Free Tour (Map p30, B2; ☎495-222 3466; www.moscowfreetour.com; Nikolskaya ul 4/5; guided walk free, paid tours from €31) Enthusiastic guides offer a free introductory walk around Red Square and Kitay Gorod, as well as thematic tours that you have to pay for.

Best St Petersburg Walking Tours

Peterwalk Walking Tours (☎812-943 1229; http://peterswalk.com; from ₽1320) Going for more than 20 years, Peter Kozyrev's innovative and passionately led tours are highly recommended as a way to see the city with knowledgeable locals.

Sputnik Tours (☎499-110 5266; www.sputnik8.com; price varies) This online tour agency is one with a difference: they act as a market place for locals wanting to give unique tours of their own city.

Placemates (☎925 845 3747; http://placemates.ru; prices vary) This online portal connects visitors with locals running a variety of tours and interesting experiences around the city.

Cruising the Moscow River

VB Excursions (☏ 812-380 4596; www.vb-excursions.com) Offers excellent thematic walking tours with clued-up students on themes including Dostoevsky and Revolutionary St Petersburg.

St Petersburg Free Tour (http://petersburgfreetour.com) The central offering of this tour company is its daily free city tour, but the company has plenty of other reasonably priced tours on offer.

Best Boat Tours in Moscow

Capital Shipping Co (ССК, Столичная Судоходная Компания; ☏ 495-225 6070; www.cck-ship.ru; adult/child 1hr cruise ₽900/700, 2-day pass ₽2400/2000) Ferries ply the Moscow River from May to September; board at one of six docks for a cruise ranging from one to two hours.

Radisson River Cruises (www.radisson-cruise.ru; adult/child from ₽750/550; Ⓜ Kievskaya) Operates big river boats that cart 140 people up and down the Moscow River from the dock in front of the hotel and from the dock in Gorky Park.

Best Boat Tours in St Petersburg

Anglo Tourismo (☏ 8-921-989 4722; http://anglotourismo.com; 27 nab reki Fontanki; 1hr cruise adult/student ₽1900/900; Ⓜ Gostiny Dvor) The main operator to run tours with commentary in English.

City Tour (☏ 812-648 1228; https://citytourspb.ru; day pass adult/child ₽700/300) Offers a 'hop on, hop off' boat tour around the main rivers and canals.

Best Bike Tours

Moscow Bike Tours (☏ 8-916-970 1419; www.moscowbiketours.com; 2½hr tour US$40-60) On these tours, you'll enjoy great views of Moscow. Day and evening rides offered, with an extended tour available on weekends.

Peterwalk Walking Tours (☏ 812-943 1229; http://peterswalk.com; from ₽1320) The best established bike tour in St Petersburg, with both daytime and night-time options offered three times a week.

Best
Eating

In recent years Moscow and St Petersburg have blossomed into culinary capitals. Foodies will be thrilled by the dining options, from old-fashioned *haute-russe* to contemporary 'author cuisine'. The ban on imported foodstuffs means that chefs are finding innovative ways to utilise local ingredients, rediscovering ancient cooking techniques and inventing new ones in the process. And diners are eating it up. Literally.

Russian Cuisine

Russian food, it's fair to say, has an image problem. It's true: if you're not careful you can easily end up with dill-smothered soups, under-seasoned and over-cooked meats, and salads that are more mayonnaise than vegetable.

But fret not: there is great Russian cooking to be had. Russian chefs have been rediscovering their own culinary history, and have been slowly moving away from the dozen standard offerings that are ubiquitous on the country's menus. They're preparing rarer or even forgotten dishes, cooked in innovative ways and combined with herbs and fresh, organic vegetables. Economic sanctions on food products from the EU have given a boost to local providers, with some places making a virtue of farm-to-table dining principles.

Cook Like a Local

If you love Russian food, you can learn to make it yourself. **Taste of Russia** (📞 8-929-694 3797; www.taste russia.ru; bldg 4, Kazarmenny per 3; 3hr course ₽3500, market tour ₽1500; Ⓜ Kurskaya) offers courses in English, as well as market tours, wine tastings and special children's classes. Cooking courses take place in the evening, when you prepare the meal, then eat it together.

Best Eating in Moscow

Delicatessen Eat, drink and chat at Moscow's smartest and friendliest gastropub. (p47)

Café Pushkin Moscow's long-standing favourite for traditional Russian food delights in an aristocratic mansion. (p48)

Khachapuri A casual, contemporary place for the eponymous Georgian speciality. (p47)

Kitayskaya Gramota A very serious take on Cantonese cooking in a playful, ironic environment. (p80)

Lavka-Lavka Delicacies straight from local farms cooked by a creative chef. (p47)

Traditional borsch soup

Twins Two contrasting perspectives create a singular dining experience. (p47)

Best Eating in St Petersburg

EM Restaurant Contemporary Russian dining at its very best. (p119)

Cococo Culinary creativity runs rampant with plenty of local ingredients. (p103)

Gräs x Madbaren Scandi-cool meets Russian locavore at this hip central restaurant. (p102)

Yat Traditional charm in a country-cottage environment moments from the Hermitage. (p102)

Duo Gastrobar Superstylish fusion food in an equally smart environment. (p129)

Koryushka Stunning Neva views and a great menu featuring St Petersburg's beloved fish speciality. (p144)

Best Caucasian Food in Moscow

Khachapuri Refreshingly affordable, but still delicious Georgian fare. (p47)

Elardzhi Traditional Georgian fare, served in a comfortable but cool courtyard setting. (p67)

Darbazi This Georgian place goes beyond the standards. (p79)

Levon's Highland Cuisine Armenia's answer to street food. (p79)

Mizandari A classy, inexpensive place in Red October. (p66)

Best Russian Food in St Petersburg

Banshiki Serving up a huge variety of nostalgic dishes with a contemporary touch. (p130)

Gogol Conjures up postrevolutionary urban style with fine Russian home cooking. (p102)

Staraya Derevnya Family-run hideaway with intimate atmosphere and delicious meals. (p144)

Severyanin Experience old-fashioned elegance at this top choice for Russian cuisine. (p118)

Best
Drinking &
Nightlife

Drinking is a favourite national pastime in Russia, and modern Moscow and St Petersburg offer venues for every occasion, mood and season. Former factories have been converted into nightclubs; leafy courtyards contain beer gardens; and communal apartments now serve as cosy cafes. Pedestrian streets are hot spots for strollers and drinkers.

Vodka

The word 'vodka' is the diminutive of the Russian word for water, *voda,* so it means something like 'a wee drop'. Most often vodka is tipped down in swift shots, often followed by a pickle. In recent years, drinking cocktails has become more fashionable, and there are many appealing cocktail bars around town.

Beer

Many visitors to Russia are surprised to learn that *pivo* (beer) is the most popular alcoholic drink in the cities. The market leader is Baltika, which makes no fewer than 12 excellent brews. Craft beer has also become popular in recent years, and there's no shortage of microbreweries and speciality beer bars offering a fine selection.

Sparkling Wine

Russians traditionally drink sparkling wine, or *shampanskoe,* to toast special occasions and to sip at the theatre. It tends to be sickeningly sweet: look for the label that says *sukhoe* (dry). Nowadays, the cities have some classy wine bars, where well-heeled customers drink fine vintages, mostly from Europe.

Best for Beer

Redrum Hitting all the right notes with its range of craft beers. (p132)

Top Hops Riverside bar with a regularly changing menu of 20 beers on tap. (p103)

Beer Boutique 1516 Heaven for craft-beer lovers on Vasilyevsky Island. (p120)

Glavpivmag A long bar with dozens of hard-working taps make this beer central. (p51)

Jawsspot Msk A Yekaterinburg favourite with views of Lubyanskaya pl. (p34)

Best for Wine

Dom 12 Warm up with a glass of vino in these cosy quarters. (p70)

Big Wine Freaks Offering an excellent variety of

wines, tasty snacks and live music. (p145)

32.05 The garden setting is begging for a glass of Bordeaux. (p50)

Best for Cocktails

Time-Out Rooftop Bar Speciality cocktails for every hour of the day with views of the Moscow skyline. (p49)

Dead Poets Bar Grown-up cocktail bar with plush upholstery and a fanatical approach to mixology. (p132)

Delicatessen The 'pub' part of this gastropub mixes a killer cocktail. (p47)

Borodabar Be sure to be sporting at least stubble when you visit the hip 'beard bar'. (p103)

Commode Clink glasses in this stylish St Petersburg bar where the bill depends on the time you spend here. (p132)

Best for Coffee

Coffee 22 Could this be the zenith of hipster cafes in St Petersburg? We think so. (p103)

Coffee Bean It was the first coffee chain in Moscow – it's still one of the best. (p81)

Art Lebedev Cafe Studio An art-filled nook for stylish coffee drinkers in the capital. (p51)

Best for Dancing

Gipsy Modern nomads' gathering on the roof of Moscow's former chocolate factory. (p70)

Mandarin Combustible Drinking and dancing all night long in the capital. (p34)

Griboyedov This long-running bunker club remains a perennial favourite for clubbers in St Petersburg. (p132)

Best Summer Cafes

Le Boule Proof that alcohol and sports are compatible – cider and pétanque at Gorky Park. (p70)

32.05 A perfectly lovely place in the Hermitage Gardens. (p50)

Dyuni Come and join the fun in St Petersburg's hipster sandpit. (p133)

Cafe Mart A top spot for drinks in the open air. (p50)

Best
Entertainment

The performing arts are a major drawcard: classical ballet, music and theatre are at the heart of Russian culture. For so long, that's all there was. Happily, times have changed, as directors, conductors and choreographers unleash their creative spirits. If your heart's set on Tchaikovsky, you won't be disappointed, but if you're yearning for something experimental, you'll find that too.

Opera & Ballet

Nobody has ever complained about a shortage of Russian classics at the opera and ballet. Take your pick from any of the great Russian composers, and you are guaranteed to find them on the playbill at one of the major theatres. The choreography and staging is usually traditional, but then again, that's why they're classics. If you tire of the traditional, keep your eye out for more modern productions that are also staged by some local companies.

Classical Music

It's not unusual to see talented musicians working the crowds inside the metro stations, often violinists single-handedly performing Vivaldi's *Four Seasons* and flautists whistling away at Mozart or Bach. While it's possible to hear a good show, a visit to one of the local orchestra halls is highly recommended. Both cities are home to conservatories and highly acclaimed philharmonic orchestras.

Contemporary Music

Live bands and DJs travel from other parts of Russia and all over Europe to perform in the many clubs and theatres. Summer is an especially busy concert season, with several big outdoor music festivals. Check the schedules of local clubs or look for signs advertising the biggest names.

 Top Tips

▶ Most theatres and clubs sell tickets online. Or, you can do it the old-fashioned way and buy tickets directly from the theatre box office.

▶ Unfortunately for summer visitors, many venues are closed between late June and early September.

Best Opera & Dance

Mariinsky Theatre The classic St Petersburg theatre oozes history and has a dazzling interior. (p108)

Bolshoi Theatre Watch the dancers glide across the stage in Moscow's most famous and most historic theatre. (p38)

Bolshoi Theatre (p38), Moscow

New Ballet Breaking down barriers (physically and culturally) in dance in the capital. (p81)

Mikhailovsky Theatre Another historic St Petersburg theatre in which to see top-quality ballet and opera productions. (p104)

Novaya Opera Recreating the classics in a beautiful setting in Moscow's Hermitage Gardens. (p51)

Alexandrinsky Theatre See ballet and drama on the St Petersburg stage where Chekhov's *The Seagull* premiered. (p104)

Best Classical Music

Tchaikovsky Concert Hall A huge auditorium that is home to Moscow's oldest philharmonic. (p52)

Moscow Tchaikovsky Conservatory Hosts several different professional orchestras, as well as student recitals. (p52)

Rimsky-Korsakov Conservatory Breathe in the history at this illustrious music school in St Petersburg. (p120)

Best Contemporary Music

Gazgolder Hottest spot for live indie and rock in the capital. (p82)

Svoboda Skater daters and music lovers unite at this Moscow hipster hang-out. (p51)

Kamchatka A homage to Kino's Viktor Tsoy, this club is where to see St Petersburg acts do their thing. (p145)

Fish Fabrique Nouvelle The ultimate St Petersburg music venue, this veritable institution is favoured by a bohemian crowd. (p133)

Best
For Free

Even with a weak rouble, St Petersburg and Moscow are not cheap destinations. Hotels and dining are notoriously overpriced, as are admission prices to many top-tier sights. However, budget-minded travellers can find a few bargains if they know where to look.

Free Museums & Art Centres

All state museums in Moscow are free on the third Sunday of the month. The Hermitage is free on the first Thursday of each month. Some private museums are always free.

The post-industrial art centres are free to enter (though you may pay for individual galleries or special exhibits). Spend an afternoon browsing the galleries and admiring the architectural repurposing.

Churches

Many churches contain amazing iconography and eye-popping frescoes – and most are free to enter. That said, some churches are museums, such as St Basil's Cathedral, which is not free.

Parks & Estates

Maybe it's no surprise that parks do not charge an admission fee: the surprise is what you'll find inside. Nowadays, parks offer everything from dance classes to drumming circles – much of which is free of charge.

At some country estates you pay to enter the museums, but seeing the beautiful grounds and churches costs nothing.

Best Free Tours

Moscow Free Tour This highly rated outfit offers a free daily walking tour, led by knowledgable and extremely enthusiastic guides. (p160)

St Petersburg Free Tour A free city tour departs every morning from Alexander Column. (p161)

Moscow Greeter Volunteer 'greeters' – local residents – show visitors their favourite places in the city. Donations accepted. (p160)

Best Free Soviet Nostalgia

Lenin's Mausoleum Don't pay money, just pay your respects. This is one of Moscow's most wacky and wonderful (and free) things to do. (p29)

Lenin's Mausoleum (p29), Kremlin, Moscow

Moscow Metro (p150)
So it's not quite free. But it only costs ₽55 to ride the metro, which is an amazing amalgamation of art museum, history lesson and mass-transit system. St Petersburg's metro is also nothing to sneeze at. (p150)

Best Art Centres

Winzavod This former wine-bottling factory now contains art galleries and boutiques, with plenty to see for free. (p74)

Loft Project ETAGI It costs nothing to enter this former bread factory and see what they're making here now. (p128)

Best Free Churches

Cathedral of Christ the Saviour The ultimate in grandiosity – no charge for gawking. (p64)

Alexander Nevsky Monastery The grounds and church are free, though you'll pay to enter the cemeteries. (p124)

Novodevichy Cemetery Opposite situation: the convent charges an admission to the grounds, but you can wander the cemetery for no charge. (p66)

Best Parks

Gorky Park Has an open-air cinema and an observatory, both of which are free of charge. (p58)

Park Zaryadye Free admission to the park, if not all the exhibits. (p33)

New Holland Listen to concerts, see outdoor exhibits or just lounge on the grass at this newly revamped island park. (p118)

Summer Garden Gorgeous manicured gardens with elaborate, wrought ironworks. (p101)

Best
For Kids

Filled with icons and onion domes, Russia might not seem like an appealing destination for kids, but you'd be surprised. In St Petersburg and Moscow, little people will find museums, parks, theatres and even restaurants that cater especially to them.

Museums & Attractions

Most sights and museums offer reduced-rate tickets for children up to 12 or 18 years of age. Kids younger than five are often free of charge. Look out for family tickets.

Outdoor Fun

Even in winter, there are plenty of chances to get outside for fresh air and exercise. With dozens of parks and gardens, Moscow and St Petersburg both have plenty of space for kids to let off steam – many parks have excellent playgrounds.

Best Kids' Museums

Grand Maket Rossiya

An epic model village of Russia's greatest sights, located on the outskirts of St Petersburg. (p147)

Central Naval Museum

This St Petersburg classic contains a superb collection of model boats. (p116)

Central Museum of the Armed Forces

You might not let your children play with guns, but how about tanks, trucks and missiles at this Moscow museum? (p45)

Museum of Soviet Arcade Machines

Find out what it was like to be a kid in the Soviet Union. Outlets in both cities. (p44)

Kunstkamera

Some children will delight in this ghoulish St Petersburg museum, but it's not for everyone. (p116)

☑ **Top Tips**

▶ Many restaurants host 'children's parties' on Saturday and Sunday afternoons, offering toys, games, entertainment and supervision for kids while their parents eat.

▶ The metro might be fun for young ones, but be careful during rush hour, when trains and platforms are packed.

▶ Both Lingo Taxi (p176) and **Detskoe Taxi** (Детское Такси; ☎ 495-765 1180; www. detskoetaxi.ru) will look out for your children, offering smoke-free cars and child seats upon request.

Grand Maket Rossiya (p147), St Petersburg

Best Outdoor Fun

Gorky Park Great fun for kids of all ages, with activities to entertain all comers. (p58)

New Holland St Petersburg's best central park for kids, with a great playground, a wooden model of a frigate to climb around, a giant chess set and free pétanque (a form of boules). (p118)

Park Zaryadye Moscow's newest park has plenty of interactive exhibits to capture kids' attention. (p33)

Kirovsky Islands Amusement parks, boats and bikes for hire,

and lots of open space make this network of park islands a great outdoors option – just a short journey from the centre of St Petersburg. (p142)

Hermitage Gardens It's not big, but there's enough room to run, as well as a great playground for the youngest set at this popular central Moscow park. (p46)

Best Kid-friendly Restaurants

Elardzhi Kids can frolic in the courtyard with playground and petting zoo. (p67)

Zoom Café Board games and cuddly toys make your kids feel right at home. (p101)

Yat Fabulous kids' play area with pet rabbits to feed. (p102)

Teplo The restaurant is full of unexpected props, from table football to a children's playroom. (p118)

Sadko There's a great children's room and a full children's menu to boot, so families are very well catered for. (p118)

Professor Puf A well-stocked playroom and plenty of kid-friendly food items. (p67)

Best
Shopping

Don't come to St Petersburg or Moscow looking for bargains. Do come looking for creative and classy clothing and jewellery by local designers; an innovative art scene; high-quality handicrafts, linens, glassware and folk art; and unusual souvenirs that you won't find anywhere else.

Fashion

Beware of sticker shock when you check out the up-and-coming fashion industry. A few local designers have blazed a trail, inventing sophisticated and stylish fashions, which you can try on at boutiques in both Moscow and St Petersburg.

Arts & Crafts

Both cities heave with shops and stalls selling that most archetypal souvenir of Russia, the *matryoshka* (nesting dolls). Other traditional souvenirs include amber jewellery, painted wooden eggs, vodka and porcelain.

Textiles

Russia's cool, moist summers and fertile soil are ideal for producing flax, the fibre used to manufacture linen. This elegant, durable fabric is respectfully known in Russia as 'His Majesty Linen'. High-quality linen products such as tablecloths, bed covers and even clothing are still manufactured in Russia – and prices are lower than their Western counterparts.

Best Shopping in Moscow

Flacon Browse the output of contemporary creatives at Moscow's equivalent of Portobello Rd, London. (p50)

Izmaylovsky Market A sprawling souvenir market. (p82)

Khokhlovka Original Unusual and controversial clothes from a co-op of young designers. (p83)

Association of Artists of the Decorative Arts Who knows what you might find in this crowded collection of shops? (p61)

Best Shopping in St Petersburg

Taiga This cool collection of shops and businesses just moments from the Hermitage is well worth exploring. (p105)

Udelnaya Fair Find the gems among the junk at this amazing, sprawling place. (p145)

Kupetz Eliseevs Glam deli and confectioners that's great for edible gifts. (p104)

Rediska Eye-catching arts and crafts made in-house or produced by St Petersburg artisans. (p121)

Survival Guide

Before You Go   **174**

When to Go 174
Book Your Stay. 174

Arriving in Moscow   **175**

From Sheremetyevo 175
From Domodedovo 175
From Vnukovo 176
From Leningrad Station 176

Getting Around Moscow   **176**

Metro 176
Taxi. 176

Arriving in St Petersburg   **177**

From Pulkovo International Airport. . . 177
From Finland Station. 177
From Moscow Station 177
From Sea Port 177

Getting Around St Petersburg   **177**

Metro 177
Taxi 178

Essential Information   **178**

Business Hours 178
Electricity 178
Money 178
Public Holidays 178
Safe Travel 179
Tourist Information 179
Travellers with Disabilities 179
Visas 180

Language   **181**

Survival Guide

Before You Go

When to Go

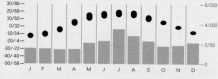

Moscow

°C/°F **Temp**
30/86 —
20/68 —
10/50 —
0/32 —
-10/14 —
-20/4 —
-30/-22 —
-40/-40 —
-50/-58 —
J F M A M J J A S O N D

Rainfall inches/mm
— 6/150
— 4/100
— 2/50
— 0

➡ Spring
Standout season to
visit. The first two weeks
of May are filled with
parades and fireworks
(though many residents
leave town).

➡ Summer
Pleasant but humid. Long
hours of sunlight bring
out revellers, especially
during White Nights in St
Petersburg.

➡ Autumn
The weather is lovely and
the cultural calendar is
busy in September and
October.

➡ Winter
Long, cold and dark, but
beautiful. The first week
of January is a festive
holiday period.

Book Your Stay

➡ It is essential to reserve
at least a month in advance
for accommodation during
the White Nights in St
Petersburg (late May to
early July).

➡ Booking online via a
hotel's website is usually
the cheapest method, as
most hotels post their
best rates online.

Best Budget

Godzillas Hostel (www.
godzillashostel.com) The
long-standing Moscow
favourite that's more of a
travellers' social club than
hostel.

Loft Hostel 77 (www.hostel
-77.com) Friendly service in
an urban chic setting in
central Moscow.

Soul Kitchen Hostel
(www.soulkitchenhostel.com)
This gorgeous hostel is
well located in central St
Petersburg and it's lots of
fun to stay.

Baby Lemonade Hostel (http://babylemonade. epoquehostels.com) Psychedelic design and a friendly environment with great *Piter* views from the roof.

Best Midrange

Bulgakov Mini-Hotel (www.bulgakovhotel.com) Literary-themed accommodation in an excellent location on the Arbat.

Danilovskaya Hotel (www. danilovsky.ru) Comfortable accommodation on the grounds of a Moscow monastery.

Hotel de Paris (www. cityhotelgroup.ru) Central, stylish and reasonably priced in the capital.

Rachmaninov Antique Hotel (www.hotelrachmaninov.com) A winner on all fronts, this smart place is an insider's top choice for St Petersburg.

Hotel Indigo (www. indigospb.com) Breathing new life into an old St Petersburg building, this superb transformation is an excellent choice.

Tradition Hotel (www. traditionhotel.ru) This charming Petrograd Side hotel is a consistent traveller favourite due to its helpful staff.

Best Top End

Hotel Baltschug Kempinski (www.kempinski-moscow.com) Ultimate luxury in the historic hotel facing the Kremlin across the river.

Hotel National (www. national.ru) Artistic and historic, the National offers a uniquely Moscow experience.

Russo Balt Hotel (www. russo-balthotel.com) Intimate, elegant and indulgent accommodation just off the Arbat.

Belmond Grand Hotel Europe (www.belmond.com) The classic St Petersburg luxury hotel, the Europe is the choice of kings and presidents.

Hotel Astoria (www.rocco fortehotels.com) A wonderfully modernised classic luxury hotel full of history in a prime location facing St Isaac's Cathedral.

Official State Hermitage Hotel (www. thehermitagehotel.ru) A dazzling affair dripping with Italian marble and chandeliers.

Arriving in Moscow

From Sheremetyevo

➡ Located in Moscow, **Sheremetyevo** (Шереметьево; ☎495-578 6565; www.svo.aero) international airport is about 30km northwest of the city centre.

➡ The **Aeroexpress Train** (☎8-800-700 3377; www. aeroexpress.ru; one way ₽420; ⊙6am-midnight) makes the 35-minute trip between Sheremetyevo (located next to Terminal E) and Belorussky vokzal every half-hour from 5.30am to 12.30am.

From Domodedovo

➡ About 48km south of Moscow, **Domodedovo** (Домодедово; ☎495-933 6666; www.domodedovo. ru) international airport is the largest and most efficient airport serving the city.

➡ The Aeroexpress Train leaves Paveletsky vokzal every half-hour between 6am and midnight for the 45-minute trip to Domodedovo.

From Vnukovo

➜ About 30km south-west of Moscow, **Vnu-kovo** (Внуково; ☎495-937 5555; www.vnukovo.ru) international airport serves most flights to/from the Caucasus, Moldova and Kaliningrad, as well as domestic flights and a smattering of flights to Europe.

➜ The Aeroexpress Train makes the 35-minute run from Kievsky vokzal to Vnukovo airport every hour from 6am to 11pm.

From Leningrad Station

➜ Located at busy Komsomolskaya pl, **Leningrad Station** (Ленинградский вокзал; http://leningradsky.dzvr.ru; Komsomolskaya pl; ☎; Ⓜ Komsomolskaya) is your point arrival from St Petersburg. Note that sometimes this station is referred to on timetables and tickets by its former name, Oktyabrsky (Октябрьский).

➜ Nearby Komsomolskaya metro station gives you easy access to anywhere in Moscow.

Getting Around Moscow

Metro

➜ The **Moscow Metro** (www.mosmetro.ru; per ride ₽55) is by far the easiest, quickest and cheapest way of getting around. Plus, many of the elegant stations are marble-faced, frescoed, gilded works of art. The 150-plus stations are marked outside by large 'M' signs.

➜ The trains are generally reliable: you will rarely wait on a platform for more than three minutes.

➜ Posted maps are generally in Cyrillic and Latin script, although the signs are usually only in Cyrillic. The carriages also have maps inside that show the stops for that line in both Roman and Cyrillic letters.

➜ Interchange stations are linked by underground passages, indicated by *perekhod* signs, usually blue with a stick figure running up the stairs. Be aware that when two or more lines meet, the intersecting stations often (but not always) have different names.

➜ The metro is still the capital's best bargain. One ride is ₽55, but you will save time and money if you buy multi-ride tickets (eg 20 rides for ₽720).

➜ The metro runs from 5.30am to 1.30am. It's always busy on working days, and often packed during rush hours.

Taxi

➜ These days, most people use apps – such as **Yandex.Taxi** (Яндекс.Такси; https://taxi.yandex.com) – to order a cab. This eliminates the language-barrier issue to an extent, given both parties know the precise departure and destination address.

➜ You can also order an official taxi by phone or book it online. Normally, the dispatcher will ring you back within a few minutes to provide a licence number of the car. Some reliable companies offer online scheduling:

Citymobil (☎495-500 5050; www.citymobil.com)

Lingo Taxi (www.lingotaxi.com) Promises English-speaking drivers (and usually delivers).

New Yellow Taxi (Новое жёлтое такси; ☎495-940 8888; www.nyt.ru)

Arriving in St Petersburg

From Pulkovo International Airport

➡ Most travellers arrive in St Petersburg at **Pulkovo** (LED; ☑ 812-337 3822; www.pulkovoairport.ru; Pulkovskoye sh), 23km south of the city.

➡ This terminal building, which opened in 2014, and still confusingly referred to as Terminal 1, handles all domestic and international flights and is St Petersburg's only airport.

From Finland Station

➡ Trains from Helsinki arrive at the **Finland Station** (Финляндский вокзал; finlyandsky vokzal; www.finlyandsky.dzvr.ru; pl Lenina; M Ploshchad Lenina).

➡ From here you can connect to anywhere in the city by metro from the Ploshchad Lenina station (line 1) on the square outside the station.

From Moscow Station

➡ If you're arriving from Moscow, you'll come to the **Moscow Station** (Moskovsky vokzal; Московский вокзал; www.moskovsky-vokzal.ru; Nevsky pr 85; M Ploshchad Vosstaniya), in the city centre.

➡ There are two metro stations close by: pl Vosstaniya (line 1) and Mayakovskaya (line 3). To get here (you can enter both stations through one building) turn left outside the main entrance to the Moscow Station, and the exit is on the side of the building on Ligovsky pr.

From Sea Port

➡ If you're arriving by ferry from Stockholm, Tallinn or Helsinki then you'll arrive at the **Sea Port** (Морской вокзал; ☑ 812-337 2060; www.mvokzal.ru; pl Morskoy Slavy 1) in the southern corner of Vasilyevsky Island. It's not served by the metro, so your easiest way into the city centre is to take a taxi.

➡ Drivers wait outside the terminal or you can order a taxi by phone app; fares average ₽200 to ₽400 depending on where in the centre you want to go.

Getting Around St Petersburg

Metro

➡ The **metro** (☑ 800 350 1155; www.metro.spb.ru; ⏱ 6am-12.45am) is a very efficient five-lined system. The network of some 70 stations is most usefully employed for travelling long distances, especially connecting the suburbs to the city centre.

➡ Look for signs with a big blue 'M' signifying the entrance to the metro.

➡ The flat fare for a trip is ₽45; you'll have to buy an additional ticket if you are carrying a significant amount of baggage.

➡ A smart card (₽60) is good for multiple journeys to be used over the course of a fixed time period – for example, 10 trips in seven days for ₽355. Their main advantage is that you won't have to line up to buy tickets – the ticket counters can have very long lines during peak hours.

➡ The metro system is fully signed in English, so it's quite easy to use, even for first-timers in Russia.

Taxi

➡ Taxi apps, such as Gett and Yandex Taxi, are all the rage in St Petersburg and they've brought down the prices of taxis in general, while improving the service a great deal.

➡ Aside from the apps, the best way to get a taxi is to order it by phone. Operators will usually not speak English, so unless you speak Russian, ask your hotel reception to call a taxi for you. Some recommended companies:

Peterburgskoe Taksi 068 (☎812-324 7777, in St Petersburg 068; www. taxi068.ru)

Taxi-4 (☎812-333 4333; www.taxi-4.ru)

Taxi Blues (Такси-Блюз; ☎812-321 8888; www. taxiblues.ru)

Taxi 6000000 (☎812-600 0000; http://6-000-000.ru)

Essential Information

Business Hours

Government offices 9am or 10am to 5pm or 6pm weekdays.

Banks and other services 9am to 6pm weekdays; shorter hours Saturday.

Shops 10am to 8pm daily. Department stores and food shops have longer hours.

Restaurants Noon to midnight daily.

Museums 10am or 11am to 6pm Tuesday to Sunday. Many museums have instituted evening hours one day a week, usually Thursday. Opening hours vary widely, as do the museums' weekly days off.

Electricity

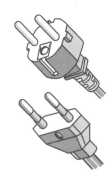

220V/50Hz

Money

➡ Even if prices are listed in US dollars or euros, you will be presented with a final bill in roubles.

➡ ATMs linked to international networks are all over Moscow – look for signs that say bankomat (банкомат).

➡ Credit cards are commonly accepted, but Americans may have some difficulty if they do not have a 'chip and pin' credit card. This is more of a problem at shops than at hotels and restaurants.

➡ Inform your bank or credit-card provider of the dates you'll be travelling in Russia, to avoid a situation where the card is blocked.

Public Holidays

New Year's Day 1 January

Russian Orthodox Christmas 7 January

International Women's Day 8 March

International Labour Day/Spring Festival 1 and 2 May

Victory (1945) Day 9 May

Russian Independence 12 June

**ay of Reconciliation
nd Accord (formerly
evolution Day)**
November

afe Travel

- As in any big city, be on
uard against pickpock-
ts, especially around
ain stations and in
rowded metro cars.

- Always carry a photo-
opy of your passport
nd visa. If stopped by
member of the police
orce, it is perfectly ac-
eptable to show a
hotocopy.

- Due to legislation crimi-
alising the 'promotion of
omosexuality' to minors,
vels of homophobia
re higher now than they
ave been for some time.
GBTIQ travellers are ad-
ised to remain discreet.

- There is an ongoing
pidemic of racist attacks
St Petersburg. If you
ok very obviously non-
ussian, it's a good idea
avoid the suburbs and
ake taxis at night.

ourist Information

iscover Moscow
ttps://um.mos.ru/en/
scover-moscow) A com-
rehensive site organised
y the City of Moscow.

Dos & Don'ts

Russians are sticklers for formality, and also
rather superstitious. Follow these tips to avoid
faux pas.

➡ **Visiting homes** Shaking hands across the
threshold is considered unlucky; wait until you're
fully inside. Remove your shoes and coat on entering. Always bring a gift. If you give flowers, make
sure they're an odd number – even numbers of
blooms are for funerals.

➡ **Religion** Women should cover their heads and
bare shoulders when entering a church. In some
monasteries and churches it's also required that
they wear a skirt – wraps are usually available at
the door. Men should remove hats in church and
not wear shorts.

➡ **Eating & Drinking** Russians eat resting their
wrists on the table edge, with fork in left hand and
knife in the right. Vodka toasts are common at
meals – it's rude to refuse to join in and traditional
(and good sense) to eat after each shot.

Moscow Tourist Hotline
(☎8-800-220 0001, 8-800-
220 0002, 495-663 1393)

**Tourist Information Bu-
reau** (☎812-303 0555, 812-
242 3909; http://eng.ispb.info;
Sadovaya ul 14/52; ☻10am-
7pm Mon-Sat; Ⓜ Gostiny Dvor)
Maps, tours, information
and advice for travellers in
St Petersburg.

Travellers with
Disabilities

➡ Inaccessible transport,
lack of ramps and lifts,
and no centralised policy

for people with physical
limitations make Russia a
challenging destination for
travellers with restricted
mobility.

➡ Toilets are frequently
accessed from stairs in
restaurants and museums;
distances are great; public
transport can be extremely
crowded; and many foot-
paths are in a poor condition and are hazardous
even for the fully mobile.

➡ This situation is
changing (albeit slowly),
as buildings undergo
renovations and become

Money-Saving Tips

➡ If you plan to use the metro a lot, buy multi-ride tickets to save money.

➡ Eat set business lunches in restaurants, which are great value and very filling. Many other places offer a discount of around 20% on all bills for meals between noon and 4pm Monday to Friday.

➡ Book in good time for the theatre, opera and ballet to get the best choice of seats and to not be limited to the most expensive.

➡ Treat yourself to a stay at a business or luxury hotel on weekends, when rates drop substantially.

more accessible. Most up-market hotels (especially Western chains) offer accessible rooms and have lifts, and the Hermitage is also now fully accessible.

➡ Download Lonely Planet's free Accessible Travel guide from http://lptravel.to/AccessibleTravel.

Visas

Nearly all visitors need a visa, which will require an invitation. Tourist visas are generally single entry and valid for up to 30 days.

Visa-free Travel
➡ Passport holders of a very few countries enjoy the positive luxury of 30- to 90-day visa-free travel.

➡ Those arriving by cruise ship and ferry in St Petersburg can take advantage of a 72-hour visa-free

regime. The condition is that the passenger must purchase a tour through an officially recognised travel agency.

Types of Visas
For most travellers a tourist visa (single or double entry, valid for a maximum of 30 days) will be sufficient. If you plan to stay longer than a month, you can apply for a business visa or – if you are a US citizen – a three-year multi-entry visa.

Invitation
To obtain a visa, everyone needs an invitation, also known as 'visa support'. Hotels and hostels will usually provide invitations for their guests, sometimes for a small fee. If you are not staying in a hotel or hostel, you will

need to buy an invitation – this can be done through most travel agents or via specialist visa agencies. Prices may vary.

Application
Invitation voucher in hand, you can then apply for a visa. Wherever in the world you are applying you can start by entering details in the online form of the **Consular Department of the Russian Ministry of Foreign Affairs** (https://visa.kdmid.ru/PetitionChoice.aspx). Keep a note of the unique identity number provided for your submitted form.

Consular offices apply different fees and slightly different application rules country by country. The charge for the visa will depend on the type of visa applied for and how quickly you need it.

Registration
On arrival you need to 'register' your passport with the local authorities, if you are staying for seven days or more. Your hotel will normally take care of this. If you're not staying at a hotel, you can usually do it at a local travel agency or visa support centre. If you are staying for fewer than seven working days, there is no need to register.

Language

Russian belongs to the Slavonic language family and is closely related to Belarusian and Ukrainian. It has more than 150 million speakers within the Russian Federation and is used as a second language in the former republics of the USSR, with a total number of speakers of more than 270 million people.

Russian is written in the Cyrillic alphabet, and it's well worth the effort familiarising yourself with it so that you can read maps, timetables, menus and street signs. Otherwise, just read the coloured pronunciation guides given next to each Russian phrase in this chapter as if they were English, and you'll be understood. The stressed syllables are indicated with italics.

To enhance your trip with a phrasebook, visit **lonelyplanet.com**. Lonely Planet iPhone phrasebooks are available through the Apple App store.

Basics

Hello.

Здравствуйте. *zdrast·vuy·*tye

Goodbye.

До свидания. da svi·*da·*nya

Excuse me.	Простите.	pras·*ti·*tye
Sorry.	Извините.	iz·vi·*ni·*tye
Please.	Пожалуйста.	pa·*zhal·*sta
Thank you.	Спасибо.	spa·*si·*ba

You're welcome

Пожалуйста. pa·*zhal·*sta

| **Yes./No.** | Да./ Нет. | da/nyet |
| **How are you?** | Как дела? | kak di·*la* |

Fine, thank you. And you?

Хорошо, спасибо. kha·ra·*sho* spa·*si·*ba
А у вас? a u vas

What's your name?

Как вас зовут? kak vas za·*vut*

My name is ...

Меня зовут ... mi·*nya* za·vut ...

Do you speak English?

Вы говорите
по-английски? vi ga·va·*ri·*tye
pa·an·*gli·*ski

I don't understand.

Я не понимаю. ya nye pa·ni·*ma·*yu

Eating & Drinking

I'd like to reserve a table for...

Я бы хотел/ ya bih khat·*yel*/
хотела khat·*ye·*la
заказать za·ka·*zat'*
столик *sto·*lik
на ... (m/f) na ...

two people

двоих dva·*ikh*

eight o'clock

восемь часов *vo·*sim' chi·*sof*

What's in that dish?

Что входит в это shto *fkho·*dit v e·ta
блюдо? *blyu·*da

I don't eat ...

Я не ем ... ya nye yem ...

Please bring the bill.

Принесите, pri·ni·*sit·*ye
пожалуйста, счёт. pa·*zhal·*sta shot

Shopping

I need ...

Мне нужно ... mnye *nuzh·*na ...

I'm just looking.

Я просто смотрю. ya *pros·*ta smat·*ryu*

Can you show me?
Покажите,   pa·ka·*zhih*·tye
пожалуйста?   pa·*zhal*·sta

How much is it?
Сколько стоит?   *skol'*·ka *sto*·it

That's too expensive.
Это очень дорого.   *e*·ta o·*chen*'*do*·ra·ga

There's a mistake in the bill.
Меня обсчитали.   min·*ya* ap·shi·*ta*·li

Emergencies

Help!   Помогите!   pa·ma·*gi*·tye

Call ...!   Вызовите ...!   *vih*·za·vi·tye ...

  a doctor   врача   vra·*cha*

  the police   полицию   po·*li*·tsih·yu

Leave me alone!
проваливай!   pro·*va*·li·vai

There's been an accident.
Произошёл   pra·i·za·*shol*
несчастный случай.   ne·*shas*·nih *slu*·chai

I'm lost.
Я заблудился/   ya za·blu·*dil*·sa/
заблудилась. (m/f)   za·blu·*di*·las'

Where are the toilets?
Где здесь туалет?   gdye zdyes' tu·al·*yet*

I'm ill.
Я болен/больна. (m/f)   ya bo·lin/bal'·na

Time

What time is it?
Который час?   ka·*to*·rih chas

It's (10) o'clock.
(Десять) часов.   (*dye*·sit') chi·*sof*

  morning   утро   *ut*·ra

  day   день   den

  evening   вечер   *vye*·chir

  yesterday   вчера   vchi·*ra*

  today   сегодня   si·*vod*·nya

  tomorrow   завтра   *zaft*·ra

Transport & Directions

Where is ...?   Где ...?   gdye ...

What's the address?
Какой адрес?   ka·*koy* a·dris

Could you write it down, please?
напишите,   na·pi·*shi*·te.mne
пожалуйста.   pa·*zhal*·sta

Can you show me (on the map)?
Покажите мне,   pa·ka·*zhih*·tye mnye
пожалуйста   pa·*zhal*·sta
(на карте).   (na *kar*·tye)

When does it leave?
Когда отправляется?   kag·*da*
                                at·prav·*lya*·it·sa

How long does it take to get to ...?
Сколько времени   *skol'*·ka *vrye*·mi·ni
нужно ехать до ...?   *nuzh*·na ye·khat'
                                da ...

Please stop here.
Остановитесь здесь,   a·sta·na·*vit*·
                                yes' zdyes'
пожалуйста.   pa·*zhal*·sta

Does it stop at ...?
Поезд останав-   *po*·yist a·sta·nav
ливается в ...?   li·va·yit·sa v ...

  bus   автобус   af·*to*·bu

  train   поезд   *po*·ist

  tram   трамвай   tram·*va*

  trolleybus троллейбус   tra·*lyey*·bu

  first   первый   *pyer*·vih

  last   последний   pas·*lyed*·n

  platform   платформа   plat·*for*·ma

  timetable   расписание   ras·pi·*sa*·ni·y

  ticket   билет   bil·*ye*

    one-way   в один   v a·*din*
                  конец   kan·*yets*

    return   туда-   tu da
                  обратно   ob·*rat*·n

Index

See also separate subindexes for:

- 🍴 Eating p186
- 🍸 Drinking p186
- 🎭 Entertainment p187
- 🛍 Shopping p187

9th and 20th Century Art Gallery 57

A

Academy of Arts Museum 113
accommodation 174-5
airports
  Moscow 175-6
  St Petersburg 177
Alexander Nevsky Monastery 124-5
Anna Akhmatova Museum at the Fountain House 128-9
Arbat (Moscow) 54-71, **62-3**
  entertainment 71
  drinking 70-1
  food 66-8
  itineraries 55, 60-1
  shopping 71
  sights 56-9, 64-6
  transport 55
architecture 143, 159
Armoury 26-7
art (contemporary) 158
Art Muzeon & Krymskaya Naberezhnaya 64

Sights 000
Map Pages **000**

ArtPlay 74-5
Association of Artists of the Decorative Arts 61

B

ballet 166-7
Basmanny (Moscow) 72-83, **76-7**
  drinking 80-1
  entertainment 81-2
  food 78-80
  itineraries 73
  shopping 82-3
  sights 74-5, 78
  transport 73
beer 164
boat tours 161
bicycle travel 17, 161
Bolshoi Theatre 38-9
bridges 119
Bunker-42 Cold War Museum 78
Burganov House 61
business hours 178

C

Cathedral of Christ the Saviour 64, 66
cell phones 16
Central Museum of the Armed Forces 45-6
Central Naval Museum 116
Chaev Mansion 143

Chkalovskaya 138-9
Chesme Church 147
children, travel with 170-1
Chistye Prudy 78
Church of the Grand Ascension 41
classical music 166-7
Church of the Saviour on the Spilled Blood 96-7
climate 174
coffee 165
Commandant's House 137
costs 16, 180
courses
  Taste of Russia 162
currency 16
cycling 17, 161

D

dangers, see safety
Detsky Mir 44
disabilities, travellers with 179
DLT 143
Dostoevsky Museum 128
drinking 164-5, see also individual neighbourhoods, Drinking subindex
Dvortsovy most 100

E

electricity 178
entertainment 166-7, see also individual neighbourhoods, Entertainment subindex
Erarta Museum of Contemporary Art 110-11
etiquette 179
Exposition of Military Equipment 85

F

Fabergé Museum 100-1
ferry travel 177
food 69, 102, 162-3, see also individual neighbourhoods, Eating subindex
free attractions 168-9
Friendship with Peoples of Foreign Countries 60-1

G

galleries 154-5
Garage Museum of Contemporary Art 59
gay travellers 179
General Staff Building 94
Georgian cuisine 69
Gorky Park 58-9

Grand Maket
  Rossiya 147
Grand Palace 156
Gulag History
  Museum 46

H
Hermitage Gardens 46
Hermitage Storage
  Facility 142
highlights 8-11, 12-13
Historic Heart
  (St Petersburg)
  88-105, **98-9**
  drinking 103-4
  entertainment 104
  food 101-3
  itineraries 89, 152-3
  shopping 104-5
  sights 90-7, 100-1
  transport 89
history 156, 157
holidays 179
Holy Trinity Alexander
  Nevsky Lavra 125
House of Soviets 147

I
imperial history 156
International Business
  Centre 41
itineraries 14-15, 150-3,
  see also individual
  neighbourhoods
Ivan the Great Bell
  Tower 25

J
Jewish Museum &
  Centre of
  Tolerance 45

Sights 000
Map Pages 000

K
Khamovniki (Moscow)
  54-71, **62-3**
  drinking 70-1
  entertainment 71
  food 66-8
  itineraries 55
  shopping 71
  sights 56-9, 64-6
  transport 55
Kirovsky Islands 142
Kitay Gorod 31
Kitay Gorod (Moscow)
  22-35, **30**
  drinking 34
  food 32-4
  itineraries 23
  shopping 34-5
  sights 24-9, 31-2
  transport 23
Kolomna
  (St Petersburg)
  106-21, **114-15**
  drinking 120
  entertainment 120
  food 117-19
  itineraries 107
  shopping 121
  sights 108-11, 116
  transport 107
**Kremlin in
  Izmaylovo 82**
Kremlin 24-7
Kremlin (Moscow)
  22-35, **30**
  drinking 34
  food 32-4
  itineraries 23
  shopping 34-5
  sights 24-9, 31-2
  transport 23
Kudrinskaya Apart-
  ment Block 41
Kunstkamera 116

L
language 181-2
  basics 181
  directions 182
  drinking 181
  eating 181
  emergencies 182
  shopping 181-2
  time 182
  transport 182
Lenin's
  Mausoleum 29
Leuchtenberg
  House 139
LGBTIQ travellers 179
local life 12-13
Loft Project ETAGI 128
Lubyanka 78

M
Mariinsky II 109
**Mariinsky Theatre
  108-9**
Melnikov House 61
**Mendeleev
  Museum 113**
**Menshikov
  Palace 113**
Meshchansky (Moscow)
  72-83, **76-7**
  drinking 80-1
  entertainment 81-2
  food 78-80
  itineraries 73
  shopping 82-3
  sights 74-5, 78
  transport 73
metro travel
  Moscow 176
  St Petersburg 177-8
**Mikhail Bulgakov
  Museum 44-5**
mobile phones 16
money 16, 178, 180

Monument to the
  Heroic Defenders
  of Leningrad 147
Moscow Biennale of
  Contemporary
  Art 158
Moscow Free Tour 32
**Moscow Museum of
  Modern Art 44**
**Moscow Triumphal
  Arch 147**
**Museum of
  Political History
  142-4**
**Museum of
  Soviet Arcade
  Machines 44**
**Museum of the
  Defence &
  Blockade of
  Leningrad 128**
**Museum of the Great
  Patriotic War 85**
museums 154-5
music 166-7

N
Narkomfin 41
**Necropolis of Art
  Masters 125**
**Necropolis of the 18th
  Century 125**
Neva Panorama 137
Nevsky Prospekt 104
New Holland 118
**New Tretyakov
  Gallery 65**
nightlife 164-5
**Nikolsky
  Cemetery 125**
**Novodevichy
  Cemetery 66**
**Novodevichy
  Convent 66**
Novy Museum 113

**ld Stock
  Exchange 112**
pening hours 178
pera 166-7

alace Square 100
ark Pobedy 84-5, 147
ark Zaryadye 33
**ark Zaryadye
  Pavilion 31**
**eter & Paul Fortress
  136-7**
etrograd
  (St Petersburg)
  134-45, **140-1**
  drinking 145
  entertainment 145
  food 144
  itineraries 135, 138-9
  shopping 145
  sights 136-7, 142-4
  transport 135
**harmacy Museum of
  Dr Pelya 113**
iter Kayak 116
esnya (Moscow)
  36-53, **42-3**
  drinking 49-51
  entertainment 51-2
  food 46-9
  itineraries 37, 40-1
  shopping 52-3
  sights 44-6
  transport 37
ublic holidays 178-9
**ushkin Museum of
  Fine Arts 56-7**

**ed Banner Textile
  Factory 139**
ed October 64
ed Square 28-9

Rostral Columns 112
Russian 181-2
Russian Museum 100
**Ryabushinsky
  Mansion 40-1**

S
safety 179
Sennaya
  (St Petersburg)
  106-21, **114-15**
  drinking 120
  entertainment 120
  food 117-19
  itineraries 107
  shopping 121
  sights 108-11, 116
  transport 107
shopping 172, *see
  also individual
  neighbourhoods,
  Shopping subindex*
Singer Building 143
Smolny (St Petersburg)
  122-33, **126-7**
  drinking 132-3
  food 129-31
  itineraries 123
  sights 124-5, 128-9
  transport 123
southern St Petersburg
  146-7
Soviet history 157
**Soviet Monument on
  Pionerskaya ul 139**
**SS Peter & Paul
  Cathedral 137**
**St Andrew's
  Cathedral 113**
**St Basil's Cathedral
  28-9**
**St Isaac's
  Cathedral 100**
**State Hermitage
  Museum 90-5**

**State History
  Museum 32**
**State Tretyakov
  Gallery Main
  Branch 64**
stolovaya (canteens) 102
**Street Art
  Museum 142**
Strelka 112
Summer Garden 101

T
taxis
  Moscow 176
  St Petersburg 178
telephone services 16
time 16
tipping 16
**Tolstoy Estate-
  Museum 65-6**
**Tolstoy Literary
  Museum 65-6**
top sights 8-11
tourist information
  179-80
tours 160-1
transport
  Moscow 175-6
  St Petersburg 177-8
Treasure Gallery 91-2
Tverskoy (Moscow)
  36-53, **42-3**
  drinking 49-51
  entertainment 51-2
  food 46-9
  itineraries 37
  shopping 52-3
  sights 38-9, 44-6
  transport 37
Triumphal Arch 100
**Trubetskoy
  Bastion 137**
**Tryokhgornaya
  Manufaktura 41**
Twelve Colleges 113

V
Vasilyevsky Island (St
  Petersburg) 106-21,
  114-15
  drinking 120
  entertainment 120
  food 117-19
  itineraries 107, 112-13
  shopping 121
  sights 108-11, 116
  transport 107
visas 16, 180
Vosstaniya
  (St Petersburg)
  122-33, **126-7**
  drinking 132-3
  food 129-31
  itineraries 123
  sights 124-5, 128-9
  transport 123
Vyborg Sides (St
  Petersburg) 134-45,
  140-1
  drinking 145
  entertainment 145
  food 144
  itineraries 135
  shopping 145
  sights 136-7, 142-4
  transport 135

W
walks 150-3
weather 174
websites 16, 174-5
White House 41
wine 164
Winter Palace 91-2
Winzavod 74-5

Y
Yusupov Palace 116

Z

Zamoskvorechie
(Moscow) 54-71,
62-3
drinking 70-1
entertainment 71
food 66-8
itineraries 55
shopping 71
sights 56-9, 64-6
transport 55

Eating ⊗

1818 Kafe and
Bikes 117

A

AC/DC in Tbilisi 67

B

Banshiki 130
Bekitzer 130
Bien Cafe & Bar 125
Björn 68
Blok 131
Bon App Cafe 33
Bosco Cafe 34
Brasserie Most 48
Bulochnye F
Volcheka 139
Buter Brodsky 118

C

Cafe Hermitage 91
Cafe Pushkin 48
Chekhov 144
Chemodan 68
Cococo 103
Co-op Garage 117

Sights 000
Map Pages **000**

D

Darbazi 79
Delicatessen 47
Dukhan Chito-Ra 78
Duo Gastrobar 129

E

Elardzhi 67
EM Restaurant 119

F

Farsh 32
Fedya, dich! 68

G

Geografiya 131
Gogol 102
Gran Cafe
Dr Zhivago 47
Grand Coffee Mania
32-3
Gräs x Madbaren 102

J

Julia Child Bistro 119

K

Khachapuri 47
Khachapuri i Vino
129-30
Kitayskaya
Gramota 80
Koryushka 144

L

Lavka-Lavka 47
Leningradskoye
Kafe 137
Lepim i Varim 46-7
Lev y Ptichka 144
Levon's Highland
Cuisine 79
Liudi Kak Liudi 80

M

Mari Vanna 48
Marketplace 102
Mechta
Molokhovets 131
Mizandari 66-7

O

Odessa-Mama 80

P

Paninaro 139
Professor Puf 67
Pushkin
Konditerskaya 48

R

Répa, The 119
Restaurant Erarta 111
Restoran 119
Ryby Net 33-4

S

Sadko 118
Schengen 130
Severyanin 118
Staraya Derevnya 144
Stolle 46
Stolovaya No 57 34
Syrovarnya 68

T

Taste to Eat 130-1
Teplo 118
Tsurtsum Cafe 75
Twins 47

U

Ukrop 97

V

Varenichnaya
No 1 67

Voronezh 68
Vsyo na Svyom Mestye
130

Y

Yat 102

Z

Zoom Café 101-2

Drinking ⌖

32.05 50

A

Apotheke Bar 103
Art Lebedev Cafe
Studio 51

B

Bar Strelka 70
Beer Boutique 1516
120
Big Wine Freaks 145
Borodabar 103

C

Cafe Didu 81
Cafe Mart 50
Chaynaya Vysota 81
Coffee 22 103
Coffee Bean 70, 81
Commode 132

D

Dead Poets Bar 132
Dictatura Estetica 71
Dom 12 70
Dyuni 133

E

Edward's 75

F

ish Fabrique
  Nouvelle 133

G

Gipsy 70
Glavpivmag 51
Griboyedov 132

H

Hat 132

J

Jawsspot Msk 34

K

Kabinet 104

L

Le Boule 70

M

Mandarin
  Combustible 34
Mod Club 104

N

Noor / Electro 49

R

Radosti Kofe 120
Redrum 132

S

Sisters Cafe 80
Solaris Lab 120
Svoboda 51

T

Time-Out
  Rooftop Bar 49
Top Hops 103

U

Ukuleleshnaya 80
Underdog 71

Z

Ziferblat 131

Entertainment ✪

Alexandrinsky
  Theatre 104
Gazgolder 82
Gogol Centre 81
Kamchatka 145
Mikhailovsky
  Theatre 104
Moscow International
  House of Music 71
Moscow Tchaikovsky
  Conservatory 52
National
  Philharmonic of
  Russia 71
New Ballet 81
Nikulin Circus on
  Tsvetnoy Bulvar 51
Novaya Opera 51-2
Pirogi on
  Maroseyka 82
Rimsky-Korsakov
  Conservatory 120
Stanislavsky
  Electrotheatre 51
Tchaikovsky Concert
  Hall 52

Shopping ⊕

ADRESS 52
Artmuza 121
Au Pont Rouge 105
Dom Knigi 71
Flacon 50
GUM 34-5
Izmaylovsky
  Market 82
Katya Dobryakova 52
Khlebozavod 9 50
Khokhlovka
  Original 83
Kupetz Eliseevs 104-5
Naivno? Ochen! 82
Odensya Dlya
  Schastya 83
Rediska 121
Roomchik 52
Taiga 105
Transylvania 52-3
Udelnaya Fair 145
Yeliseev Grocery 53
Zaporozhets
  Heritage 50

Behind the Scenes

Send Us Your Feedback

We love to hear from travellers – your comments help make our books better. We read every word, and we guarantee that your feedback goes straight to the authors. Visit **lonelyplanet.com/contact** to submit your updates and suggestions.

Note: We may edit, reproduce and incorporate your comments in Lonely Planet products such as guidebooks, websites and digital products, so let us know if you don't want your comments reproduced or your name acknowledged. For a copy of our privacy policy visit lonelyplanet.com/privacy.

Mara's Thanks

Many thanks to my coauthors and resident Moscow experts Marc Bennetts and Leonid Ragozin. Always a pleasure to work with colleagues so insightful and well-informed. I also received useful information from Andrei Musiano and Sasha Serbina at Garage Museum of Contemporary Art and Dmitry Elovsky at Zaryadye Project, as well as Andrey Muchnik and Marina Dedozhdy. Unlimited thanks and love to мои самые любимые – Van, Shay and Jerry – for coming along for the adventure.

Leonid's Thanks

Many thanks to my Moscow friends, too numerous to be listed here, for ideas on new places and latest developments. Separate thanks to my wife Maria Makeeva for enduring the mayhem.

Simon's Thanks

Many thanks to my fellow Russia authors and to the following: Richard and Alison Stunt and family, Shannon Scarborough, Nashapigov Zaur, Dmitry Lemeshev, Vladimir Sevrinovskiy, Victor Yanchenko, Andrey Misiano, Kira Tverskaya, Peter Kozyrev, Andrey and Sasha.

Regis's Thanks

Many thanks to Tatiana and Vlad for the warm welcome in Petersburg; Peter Kozyrevfor Chkalovsky knowledge and the late-night strolling seminar; Darina Gribova for the street art tour; Vladimir, Yegor and Natasha of Wild Russia for many local recommendations; and friend and fellow author Simon Richmond for his many helpful tips. Warm thanks to Cassandra and daughters Magdalena and Genevieve for all their support.

Acknowledgements

Cover photograph, pp4-5: St Basil's Cathedral, Andrea Armellin/4Corners ©

Contents photograph: Russian nesting dolls, risteski goce/Shutterstock ©

This Book

This 1st edition of Lonely Planet's *Pocket Moscow & St Petersburg* guidebook was curated by Mara Vorhees, who also researched and wrote it along with Leonid Ragozin, Simon Richmond and Regis St Louis. This guidebook was produced by the following:

Destination Editor
Brana Vladisavljevic

Product Editors Rachel Rawling, Anne Mason

Senior Cartographers
David Kemp, Julie Sheridan

Book Designer
Virginia Moreno

Assisting Editors Judith Bamber, James Bainbridge, Michelle Bennett, Nigel Chin, Andrea Dobbin, Samantha Forge, Emma Gibbs, Jennifer Hattam, Gabrielle Innes, Helen Koehne, Christopher Pitts, Sarah

Reid, Gabrielle Stefanos, Fionnuala Twomey, Sam Wheeler

Assisting Book Designer
Meri Blazevski

Cover Researcher
Naomi Parker

Thanks to Paul Harding, Elizabeth Jones, Valentina Kremenchutskaya, Alison Lyall, Kate Mathews, Clara Monitto, Kirsten Rawlings, Kira Tverskaya

Simon Richmond

Journalist and photographer Simon has specialised as a travel writer since the early 1990s and first worked for Lonely Planet in 1999 on the *Central Asia* guide. He's long since stopped counting the number of guidebooks he's researched and written for Lonely Planet, but countries covered include Australia, China, India, Iran, Japan, Korea, Malaysia, Mongolia, Myanmar (Burma), Russia, Singapore, South Africa and Turkey. For Lonely Planet's website he's penned features on topics from the world's best swimming pools to the joys of urban sketching – follow him on Instagram (@simonrichmond) to see some of his photos and sketches.

Regis St Louis

Regis grew up in a small town in the American Midwest – the kind of place that fuels big dreams of travel – and he developed an early fascination with foreign dialects and world cultures. He spent his formative years learning Russian and a handful of Romance languages, which served him well on journeys across much of the globe. Regis has contributed to more than 50 Lonely Planet titles, covering destinations across six continents. His travels have taken him from the mountains of Kamchatka to remote island villages in Melanesia, and to many grand urban landscapes. When not on the road, he lives in New Orleans.

Our Writers

Mara Vorhees

Mara has been travelling to Moscow since it was the capital of a different country, and the ambition and dynamism of this city never ceases to surprise her. The pen-wielding traveller has contributed to dozens of Lonely Planet titles, including *Russia* and *Trans-Siberian Railway*. Her stories have appeared in *Delta Sky*, *BBC Travel*, *Vancouver Sun* and *Boston Globe*, among others. Nowadays, she often travels with her seven-year-old twins (who are crazy about Kuklachev's cats). Follow their adventures at www.havetwinswilltravel.com.

Leonid Ragozin

Leonid studied beach dynamics at the Moscow State University, but for want of decent beaches in Russia, he switched to journalism and spent 12 years voyaging through different parts of the BBC, with a break for a four-year stint as a foreign correspondent for the *Russian Newsweek*. Leonid is currently a freelance journalist focusing largely on the conflict between Russia and Ukraine (both his Lonely Planet destinations), which prompted him to leave Moscow and find a new home in Rīga.

OVER PAGE — MORE WRITERS

Published by Lonely Planet Global Limited
CRN 554153
1st edition – Mar 2018
ISBN 978 1 78701 123 6
© Lonely Planet 2018 Photographs © as indicated 2018
10 9 8 7 6 5 4 3
Printed in Singapore

Although the authors and Lonely Planet have taken all reasonable care in preparing this book, we make no warranty about the accuracy or completeness of its content and, to the maximum extent permitted, disclaim all liability arising from its use.